TRIPLE ELIMINATION TOURNAMENT

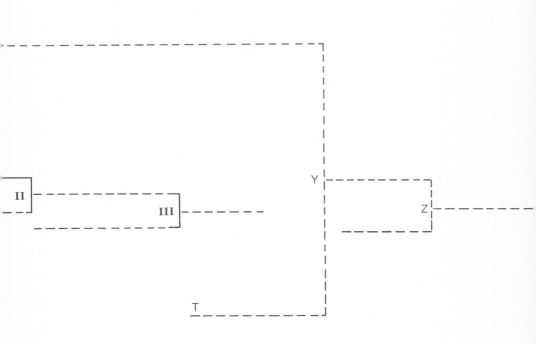

STRUCTURED INTRAMURALS

FRANCIS M. ROKOSZ

Director of Intramurals,
Wichita State University, Wichita, Kansas

1975

W. B. SAUNDERS COMPANY • Philadelphia / London / Toronto

W. B. Saunders Company: West Washington Square
Philadelphia, PA 19105

12 Dyott Street
London, WC1A 1DB

833 Oxford Street
Toronto, Ontario M8Z 5T9, Canada

Library of Congress Cataloging in Publication Data

Rokosz, Francis M

Structured intramurals.

Bibliography: p.

1. Intramural sports.   2. College sports.

I. Title.

GV710.R64   796'.07'1173   74–12918

ISBN 0–7216–7635–9

Structured Intramurals   ISBN 0-7216-7635-9

Last digit is the print number: 9   8   7   6   5   4   3   2   1

For when the One Great Scorer comes to write
    against your name,
He marks—not that you won or lost—but how
    you played the game.

PREFACE

Two general revelations are offered here, and they provide the emphases of this book. One involves the fact that the laborious nature of intramural organization and administration need not translate itself into endless pages of textbook discussion, and the other deals with the elucidation of procedures for structuring tournaments and solving tournament scheduling problems.

One fact to which any intramural director can testify is that the conduct of an intramural program encompasses many topical areas. Several of these areas, however, can be adequately discussed in short order. The reader is assumed to have a certain organization-of-sports orientation, which allows me to present the elements of effective administration in readable fashion. You, the reader, are not "snowed" with unnecessary detail. The presentation is to the point.

Absent from this textbook are pages of organizational charts and long lists of things. Programs for women, faculty, and co-ed competition are not specifically discussed because they are handled in essentially the same manner as those for men. Extramurals, outdoor recreation, and community recreation are topics not related to the concentration of this book. Only cursory treatment is made of such items as history, the organization of units of competition, the selection of proper scheduling times, the financing of the program, the handling of the budget, the procurement of equipment, and the use of facilities because I regard that information to be unimportant, found elsewhere, subject to self-analysis, or inherently obvious to the sports-minded individual.

While many intramural directors are charged with the responsibilities of handling sports clubs and scheduling unstructured recreation, those areas are not discussed here because they involve, in most cases, only the appropriate scheduling of facility use and the assignment of faculty supervision. Sports club programs which involve inter-scholastic competition require further organizational thought, but they, being extramural in nature, are not within the scope of this book.

This intramural presentation is designed to provide you with a basis for making organization and administration decisions which are applicable to any situation. This book is *not* designed to make those decisions for you. The reader must use his imagination, look past the written line, and think creatively to adapt or develop ideas to fit a particular institutional circumstance. Although my own ideas surely come through, the underlying emphasis of the discussion is on the provocation of intramural thought — not what to think, but what to think about. Only a few ideas are presented to stimulate thought on each topic. The rest is up to you as the intramural thinker.

The section on *Tournaments and Problem Solving* deals with the structuring of tournaments and the calculations which can be made to facilitate intramural scheduling. The determinations which are presented in that section will almost certainly seem involved and cumbersome at first reading. When properly learned and committed to memory, though, they become invaluable tools for the quick solution to your tournament needs.

Of course, not everything that appears in that section is particularly useful to all intramural directors. Typical concentration probably would be placed on the single elimination, double elimination, and round robin tournaments because they are used most frequently.

It is well to note that the value of tournament knowledge goes beyond that which can be directly applied to an intramural program. Institutional faculty members tend to be regarded as experts in their individual pursuits. The intramural director is often viewed as the expert in tournament construction, and he is periodically called upon for advice on that matter. An awareness and a reasonable familiarity with the subject of tournaments and problem solving is therefore essential. Since intramurals is, to some degree, a science, it seems appropriate that the director understand the structural and mathematical bases for his profession.

While the content of this book is primarily directed toward the college intramural classroom, it is by no means limited to use by students only. In particular, the comprehensive approach to the areas of tournaments, scheduling, and program evaluation lends itself as a valuable reference for intramural professionals, YMCA and YWCA people, directors of recreation and parks, and recreation directors in the armed forces.

Much of what appears in the section *Tournaments and Problem Solving* was originated by C. M. "Dutch" Sykes, Director of Intramurals at the Penn State University. I owe Dutch a great debt of gratitude for providing me with the opportunity to participate in a fine intramural program as an undergraduate, and for giving me the basis for my intramural learning. In my two years apprenticeship as his assistant, Dutch exposed me not only to the "nuts and bolts" side of intramurals, but to a philosophy of leadership which I intend to carry on.

To Dutch, this book is thereby dedicated.

CONTENTS

9

10

11

12

13

14

15

SECTION THREE: SCHEDULING AND EVALUATION

16

17

SECTION

I

ELEMENTS OF ADMINISTRATION

The Intramural
Existence

DEFINITION OF INTRAMURALS

Intramurals is a rather involved and popular enterprise. Its proper development at any institution requires a considerable commitment in time, effort, money, facilities, equipment, and staff. In light of this fact, it seems reasonable to exert some effort in determining what intramurals is, what is involved, why it exists, and what its values might be.

The meaning of the word *intramural* can be clarified by parting it into *intra* and *mural*. *Intra* means within and *mural* means wall. The term intramurals, when applied to the concerns of this book, means activities, games, and sports played among the members of the same institution. More than likely, the activities are formally organized and are conducted within the institutional grounds. Neither of these, however, is a requirement for the term to be applicable. Activities can be held anywhere and can be formally or informally directed. The necessity is that no institutional or organizational outsiders be allowed to participate.

Intramurals is usually the word used to describe all possible activities that may be conducted within an institution, but other words can be added to be more specific. Intramural athletics usually denotes the traditional activities which require physical exertion. Intramural sports may be used for a program which includes less physical games such as pool and chess. Intramural activities could include virtually any form of recreation—movies, dances, and so forth.

In contrast, extramurals indicates those activities which take place between the members of two or more institutions. It includes interscholastic athletics, competition between sports clubs or members of sports clubs, and contests between participants of different schools. The term *intermural* is sometimes used for extramurals.

For the intents of this book, intramurals involves the organization and administration of structured contests played in leagues, meets, and elimination tournaments. From the administrative point of view, it basically involves the publicizing, scheduling, organizing, supervising, and recording of events.

The intent of intramurals is that it be a voluntary program. Participation should not be mandatory because intramurals is primarily recreation and not education, although there are educational elements. Intramurals can be legitimately thought of as a competitive outlet for physical education students. It provides an opportunity for them to improve and test their skills in game or meet situations, thereby performing an informal self-evaluation. Additional educational experiences might accrue to individuals in the roles of leaders, followers, officials, coaches, and student supervisors. Hopefully, a participant also maintains or improves his sense of sportsmanship, cooperation, and the values of leisure time activity.

Benefits from intramural participation can be had in the areas of an individual's mental health, physical fitness, and social awareness. Participants experience the ups and downs of victory and defeat and, hopefully, learn to live with both. Many friends and acquaintances can be made through sports, and that is especially important to an individual who is in an unfamiliar environment.

Intramural participation should have a recreative effect on one's mental health. Vigorous play helps clear and freshen the mind, and a reasonable amount of physical activity should produce a corresponding degree of physical fitness.

Inasmuch as the values of intramural participation are clearly accepted, it serves no good purpose to dwell on them. What must be determined is why intramurals exists. The answer to that is, at least, superficially simple — it exists because students like it and want it. Why they like it and want it is surely individualized and therefore complex, but the basic reason for the existence of intramurals is that they are fun. Most students are not stimulated to play by values per se. They want the enjoyable experience which is intramurals. No justification for intramurals is needed beyond the enthusiasm displayed by its participants.

DEVELOPMENT

As with most human endeavors, the development of competitive physical activity began on an intramural basis. Whether games were played in an educational institution or just in the neighborhood, participants organized themselves. The resulting competition among students occurred, then, in informal fashion. Typically, classes of students challenged each other in activities such as baseball, rugby, and boating. A time fix puts baseball at Princeton by 1857 and boating at Yale in 1859.

Interest in intramural play often led to competition between students of different schools. That, in turn, led to an institutional emphasis on varsity athletics, which were largely sponsored by the alumni. College administrators saw the alumni interest in athletics as a financial godsend, therefore effort was centered around the physical activity of a few, and the intramural needs of student bodies at large were neglected.

However, student interest in intramural play went undaunted. Students on many campuses organized themselves by class and fraternity associations and made intramurals a standard, yearly occurrence. As student participation in intramurals increased and program activities expanded, significant conflicts arose with varsity sports programs regarding facility use.

By the early 1900s, unorganized intramurals had gotten

too big. The need for institutional control was recognized, and in 1913 official leadership was established at Ohio State and Michigan universities. Departments of intramurals were placed under the authority of individual faculty members, and the universities' total athletic programs were better coordinated as a result. Other educational institutions followed suit, particularly after World War I, when intramurals experienced a general rise in popularity.

Interest in women's intramurals appeared in the early 1920s, and many high schools began to institute intramural programs in the late 1920s.

Currently, intramural programs for men and women are well established in most institutions of higher education, but high schools in general do not have the capacity for offering students broad programs. However, the public schools have been making significant progress in recent years with the growing awareness that the recreational and competitive desires of their students must be met.

THE DIRECTOR AND HIS JOB

It doesn't take a genius to be a good intramural director. The need is for someone who has a genuine interest in his work, a background upon which to base program decisions, and the ability and flexibility to think creatively, though not necessarily innovatively.

Directing an intramural program tends to be an art rather than a science because there is little set theory to intramural programming. There are certain considerations that must be made in all programs, but no standard solutions to problems can really be identified. Each institution provides a unique setting for intramurals, and any particular situation can be handled effectively in more ways than one. In this way, intramurals becomes a system of ideas. The director simply selects and applies appropriate ideas to the identifiable aspects of intramural development. He creates his own system of ideas (the program), but the ideas he uses need not be absolutely new. A solid program can very nicely be built on the methods of others; yet one should not become complacent or think that everything worthwhile has already been developed. Peculiar situations, as well as common ones, may be best served through innovation or variation of known practice.

Although the director's initial tools of programming are those which he borrows from established programs, he may find it necessary at some time to develop new and more satisfying means of handling certain aspects of the program. However, for the most part one need only seek out current information on intramural ideas and blend them into one's own program. Numerous intramural methods can be found in books, magazines, and institutional handbooks. Most effectively, intramural people have established organizations such as the National Intramural Association and the National Intramural Sports Council, which is a division of the AAHPER; and they meet regularly to exchange and discuss ideas. Face-to-face confrontation is quite valuable because ideas can be challenged and further explained.

Most intramural programs are rather small, one-man operations. A relationship between program participation and the size of the intramural staff usually exists so that increases in participation lead to the installment of student supervisors, graduate assistants, and faculty assistants. Some of the programs at large universities are directed by staffs of as many as twenty permanent people. At those institutions where permanent intramural assistants exist, programs tend to be rather stable. When directors move on or retire, one of the assistants is named director and the program is usually carried on with few significant changes.

The majority of people who become new directors of intramurals do so as outsiders. Because there is no chain of succession at smaller schools, a new director of intramurals is commonly chosen from among the student or faculty assistants of other institutions. Whatever his previous experience, the new director usually does not have extensive knowledge of his new situation. A transition occurs for both director and institution, so the key word becomes adjustment.

It takes one or two years for a new director to get an accurate feel for the institution's situation. Although a program plan must be established, the first year is largely spent noting changes that should be made the following year for a more refined program. Further adjustments are made after the second year, and by the third year the program should have more or less stabilized. Of course, changes are made any time thereafter, as dictated by circumstances.

What is needed for maintaining student interest is program continuity. Change for the sake of change is not good.

Students feel more comfortable with a relatively stable program than one which undergoes constant or periodic fluctuation. Participants like to feel that they know what to expect from year to year. They want an orderly existence without too many questionable surprises; however, changes for the better are generally welcomed, whether initiated by students or director. Intramural participation solidifies as responsive continuity takes hold.

Taken as a whole, intramurals is an involved business. Directors generally must know something about everything, and should probably know almost everything about everything. Capabilities in student relations, general sports knowledge, and organization of schedules, meets, and internal affairs are essential. Trying to keep the rules straight of some twenty-odd sports is a job in itself. For all the apparent complexity, however, intramural administration seems quite manageable when its many considerations are viewed individually. Isolation of the specific aspects of intramural direction allows for a simplified analysis of problems and solutions. That does not mean that specific questions are answered in a vacuum. Quite often, decision-making is based on factors which cross area lines. The point is that intramural programming is not intellectually difficult. Good program decisions demand a certain amount of thought, but time-consuming effort is the primary requirement to implement the program essentials. Most of the director's time is spent in performing the necessary tasks of administration.

Just about anybody can be an intramural director, but not everybody can be a *good* intramural director. The demands of the job are such that certain inherent qualities are required of the director as a person. Perhaps most important is that the director be sincerely interested in intramurals. Ensuring that the program is well organized and fun for the students is at times a laborious task. If the director does not really enjoy intramural work, he won't consistently perform all the little duties that make a program. Intramurals tends to be an all-day, five-days-a-week job. At certain times of the year, there is little time for anything else. The proper conduct of an intramural program can wear a person down unless he enjoys spending the time in doing what needs to be done.

A director must also have a natural talent for organization. Intramural organization can be taught, of course, but it can't be effectively taught to a wall. The learner must have natural talents of his own that enable him to apply the practical theory learned in one situation to other situations.

The director's personality often plays a significant role in the establishment of an intramural program. A good deal of time is spent in working with and for people, so a pleasing personality can be a real attribute for the director in getting things done and satisfying the students' interests. As long as sound organization is employed, a program is not likely to collapse because a director has a poor personality; but a good personality usually leads to a pleasant atmosphere, and that makes intramurals more enjoyable for the participants.

It is true enough to say that a good personality does not necessarily lead to good student relations. A person with a pleasing disposition may not know how to deal with people in administrative situations, while the person with a poor personality may be able to handle students effectively. There are, no doubt, specific diplomatic techniques that can be used to handle relations with students, but the best way to associate with students is in a natural manner and without much attention paid to manipulative techniques. Students can usually tell whether a speaker believes in his own speeches or whether he's saying something just to please the listener. It is reasonably important that the students like and trust the intramural director. Real communication is thereby simplified. A further discussion of student relations appears later in this chapter.

The role of the director of intramurals within his own program usually varies with the availability of staff assistants. One-man operations, however, can be described rather accurately: the director must do everything. At one time or another, and sometimes all at once, the intramural director is a philosopher as he determines his general views of intramurals, a coordinator of activities and supporting tasks, a policy maker, an organizer and director of meets and contests, a scheduler, a supervisor of contests, a trainer of officials (sometimes an official himself), a publicity man, a secretary, a student relations man who seeks out feedback from the participants in the program, an arbitrator of disputes, an accountant and balancer of budgets, an expert in sports and sports rules, a purchaser and manager of equipment and supplies, a lawyer who must occasionally defend his policies, a statistician, a handyman who designs and repairs special devices and equipment, an author of handbooks and informational materials, a mail carrier, an errand boy, and an office occupant who is consistently available to talk with anyone who might drop in.

The development of an intramural program requires a good deal of decision making. Before the director of intramurals can make sound program decisions, he should think out his viewpoints on the various issues of intramurals and establish a general philosophy of operation. One's thoughts on the simple question of whether intramurals is education or recreation can affect the whole tone of the program as well as its specific mechanics. Assuming that finances were no factor, for instance, the employment of student or professional assistants and officials would be affected by the answer to that question.

Initial points of view need not be, and probably should not be, rigidly held. Experience tends to modify or alter one's ideas, but the most significant stimulus for change might come from the students themselves. The director's concept of virtuous intramural policy and what the kids want may be two different things. In that situation, the director must decide how to handle the conflict of interests. Shall he force-feed, negotiate a compromise, or let the students have what they want? There are any number and combinations of factors that could influence such a decision. Does the issue involved concern a fundamental or minor principle of intramurals? Is the safety of the participants a factor? Are available finances, time, assistants, and facilities a factor? How strongly do the students feel about their position? If the students' wishes are not met, will participation in the program suffer?

The matter of intramurals as education or recreation can creep into one's thinking quite often. If one considers intramurals to be largely part of the total educational flow, certain ideas could be imposed, perhaps justifiably. Policies regarding awards, point systems, and units of participation come to mind. Intramurals is supposed to be fun, though, and in light of that recreational ideal it seems likely that one would want to adjust to what the students want. Excepted are student interests which might result in safety hazards or unacceptable administrative difficulty. Whatever the case, it must be remembered that intramurals is for the students. Intramurals can be a student's most memorable college experience, so every effort should be made to satisfy his interests.

In conjunction with formulating a philosophy, an intramurals director should also determine the goals and supporting objectives of his program. Many program objectives could be cited, but there are a few goals that seem to be highly important. Decisions that dictate intramural policy should be directed toward satisfying three interrelated objectives — to increase organizational quality and program participation, and to provide participants with a pleasant experience.

Intramurals is the most fun when the best facilities, equipment, officials, and organization are employed and a pleasantly exciting atmosphere prevails. Participation should increase as quality improves, and should be more fun as the size of tournaments grows. Increases in participation often lead to an allotment of more money for intramurals, which in turn allows for improvements in organization and administration and an expansion of program offerings. One thing leads to another. The trick is to get the ball rolling in the program's favor.

THE STAFF

In those programs that warrant it, a staff must be assembled and organized. The selection of assistants can be made from the basic categories of teaching faculty, coaching faculty, graduate students, and undergraduate students. The number and type of assistants employed usually depend on available finances and the size of the program. Smaller programs might have one or two student assistants, who would probably be used to supervise contests and aid in conducting meets. Graduate assistants can be given more responsibility, such as keeping records, training and scheduling officials, and performing other tasks. Student assistants might also be placed in charge of administrating some of the less involved sports, such as tennis and golf. The assistants could schedule, supervise, record, and otherwise see that tournaments run smoothly.

Large universities might have undergradate, graduate, and faculty assistants employed in the intramural program. Their duties can be channeled in two basic ways. Each assistant could be put in complete charge of the organization and administration of one or more sports. The second method is to assign as a unit the various tasks involved in conducting every sport, so that each staff member handles either scheduling, training and scheduling of officials, managing equipment, preparing facilities, or recording results for all sports. Supervision is the responsibility of everyone and is equally shared. Which of these systems is better is a debatable question; each has its advantages and disadvantages.

There are also many combinations of ways in which to organize an intramural staff. Each director must choose the best system for his particular situation. One of the initial steps might be to hire a knowledgeable and reliable first assistant. Every intramurals director could use someone whom he can trust to think clearly and take charge of certain aspects of the program. Even in small programs, it is difficult for the director to coordinate everything that must be done. He needs responsible help to run a smooth and expert organization. The primary qualifications for all other assistants is that they be very interested in working with intramurals, and have some natural ability in relating to students. They can be given effective on-the-job training so that they can help implement the program. There is really no particular need for more than two thinkers or policy makers.

FINANCES AND FACILITIES

From the upper administration viewpoint, intramurals is a numbers game. Better facilities and increases in funds and staff usually depend upon an increase in the number of students participating in the program. The director of intramurals must somehow improve his program, using whatever means are available, in order to attract more participants. The available means improve when participation gets better.

Although participation usually leads to money, money does not always lead to significant increases in participation. Typically, intramural money is spent for payment of student assistants and officials; purchase of awards, equipment, and supplies; and publication costs. When a program is held back owing to lack of funds, increased money may permit a greater number of program offerings, which almost certainly will lead to increased participation. However, there are also situations in which participation is low because of certain institutional factors (poor facilities, most students work), even though enough money is available to offer a wide variety of activities. In those instances, money used properly results in improvements in program quality, but these might not lead to an immediate increase in participation. Certain limitations make it impossible for money to buy significant increases in student participation.

At some institutions, intramurals is not highly regarded, and the intramural budget is financed through unstable sources of funds. Combinations of gate receipts, entry fees, forfeit fees, and fund-raising gimmicks might be employed. In such cases it is difficult to plan a well balanced program. The best and most consistent means of financing a program is through a standard budget, which utilizes funds from student fees or the regular operating funds of the institution.

Intramural money is spent for the general items of personnel, equipment, and supplies. At the beginning of each year, with the budgeted figure for intramurals in hand, the director should sit down and outline the approximate expenditures for the coming year. This is not an easy undertaking, nor are the results absolutely accurate, because expenses fluctuate, as does participation, from year to year. Each anticipated expenditure should be itemized so that during the course of the year the director can keep track of overspending or underspending and make the appropriate adjustments. Adjustments can be made in several areas — deletions or additions to the program of activities, an increase or decrease in the number of contests scheduled, and an increase or decrease in the number or pay of assistants, supervisors, and officials.

Almost all intramural programs must share facilities with physical education classes, varsity sports, sports clubs, and special events. As early in the year as possible, the director should obtain a schedule of facility use from the facilities coordinator and prepare a reasonably accurate calendar of events. Scheduling conflicts are intolerable and can foul up the program.

A good many intramural programs must share equipment with others, too. The best way to handle equipment is to buy the best and have it under intramurals control. The better the equipment, the more fun is intramurals; and the more equipment that the intramural department controls, the more efficient and less troublesome can be its operation.

As much equipment as finances allow should be provided for the playing of intramural contests — rackets, balls, jerseys, and so forth. Officials should be given at least shirts and whistles. Although it is somewhat bothersome, some provision should probably be made for supplying students with equipment for free play. Careful note must be taken of who checks out equipment. Standard procedure is for the student to present his ID card before equipment is charged to him. The borrower pays for equipment broken or not returned.

STUDENT RELATIONS

The opinion was once voiced that "all there is to intra-murals is knowing how to handle people." Well, not quite, but one's abilities in relating effectively with students is highly important to the overall acceptability of an intramurals program. Sooner or later, even the best administrated programs run into trouble in the event of strained relations between students and directors.

Discussions of student relations in intramurals can be divided into two categories—formal and informal. Formal relations deal with such organized entities as the intramural council, the implementation of a student managerial system, and the corps of organization intramurals chairmen. The informal aspect relates to those instances when students and directors talk to each other in unplanned, "off the cuff" situations. Such conversations may occur in the intramural office, on the field or court of play, or elsewhere on campus.

Many schools emphasize the idea of involving students not only in the participatory aspect of intramurals, but also in the administrative aspect. Because the program is for the students, they should be involved as much as possible in the direction and promotion of their own program. Toward that end, and for practical purposes also, some programs employ systems of sport managers. Students are placed in charge of the scheduling, management, and supervision of specific program activities. Not only do the students achieve a sense of involvement in the direction of the program but they gain an educational experience and aid what might otherwise be an overworked director.

In the intramural council, there is the potential for a formal body of students that governs the program, or at least has an advisory role. Councils usually consist of representatives from all divisions of the program and, typically, they are responsible for ruling on protests and violations of the regulations, initiating program changes, and voting on changes suggested by other students or the director. Very few schools have councils which hold any real authority, however, and the relative power of councils varies widely from school to school. Some councils are strongly supported by the students and are thereby strong. Others are so ineffective and weak that they are little more than a facade. Much depends on the director's view of student participation in the governing process. He is often the one who determines the influence of the council.

The informal aspect of student relations might be described as encompassing those situations where students walk into the office and discuss, question, or complain about some intramural policy. The director's reactions to these situations is a major factor in setting the tone of the program.

The role of the director (or any staff member) in student relations is difficult to describe in a "how to do it" context. What to say to whom and when and in what specific situations to say them are lessons that cannot easily be taught in a straightforward, explanatory way. The proper handling of problems that require personal communication between directors and students is most effectively learned through the experiences of personal involvement in dealing with such problems and observation of others who are skillful in this field. With that in mind, some general observations or suggestions can be made.

Probably the most important item of concern is the atmosphere in which the intramural program exists. There is no need for the program to be run like a military operation with a no-nonsense approach and with strict, unbreakable rules. Good programs tend to be relaxed and at least reasonably flexible. When the students ask questions about certain policies or why their team can't be scheduled for play on a different night, the director should respond in a pleasant manner. There is no need for a "that's the way it is, like it or lump it" attitude. There should be good reasons for anything that is done in intramurals, and if the director can effectively communicate them to interested students, everyone should be satisfied. Should the director be unable to explain the considerations involved in making decisions, then it's time for him to reflect on the possibility of making changes.

If students make good suggestions for changes in the program, there is no reason why the director cannot seriously take them into account. Compromises go a long way toward smoothing out differences of opinion. The overall effectiveness of some programs may depend on the director's willingness and ability to compromise.

Most students just want a fair shake. What they need is the feeling that they will not be turned away gruffly when they walk into the intramural office. It's simply a matter of giving explanations when they are needed; and in that light, even the formality of an intramural council becomes somewhat superfluous.

Students sometimes fear dictatorial rule when no means for effecting change is available to them. An intramural council may provide such an outlet, or it may project the picture of confrontation rather than cooperation. All that is really needed to satisfy student desires for program input is an effective open-door policy. Anyone should be able to enter the intramural office and initiate change by simply presenting sound arguments for his proposal. Intramural councils often become unnecessary when there is a director who has an open door and is accessible for discussions with students.

It seems that relaxed informality is the key to effective relations with students who participate in the intramural program.

2

The Program of Activities

SELECTION

In general, a well regarded intramural program is said to have a balance of individual, dual, and team sports. The emphasis should be on the quality of the administrative capability to conduct the program, rather than on the quantity of offerings. The idea is to offer variety so that as many interests as possible are served.

The extent of balance, however, and the selection of sports itself depends upon several considerations, and usually, no one decision regarding the inclusion or exclusion of a program sport is made on the basis of one factor alone. A number of elements affect evaluation.

The director's philosophy influences many decisions. Essentially, he creates the atmosphere in which the program is to proceed. A philosophy of rugged competition, for example, leans toward combative sports, directly affecting the type of touch football that is played. Flag football and touch football played with few blocking restrictions can be particularly rough and bruising if not outright dangerous. Philosophies leaning toward a spirit of gentlemanly competition might result in regulations that severely limit blocking, or eliminate it completely. Some institutions have phased out football entirely and replaced it with other equally invigorating but less dangerous sports. Soccer, speedball, and angle ball (see later in this chapter) are three good substitutes.

Philosophy also affects the emphasis on individual, dual, or team sports in several ways. Activities might be chosen on the basis of their very natures. For instance, football is a team sport; chess is individual. Sports such as badminton and tennis can be played as individual or dual sports, and many sports can be programmed as either individual or individual-team. Cross-country, track and field, swimming, and wrestling are examples of the latter. In addition, some activities can be conducted as team sports even though they incorporate both individual and dual play. For example, one could conduct tennis tournaments between organizations on a team basis. With four players to a team, a match might consist of four singles matches and a doubles match.

An individual-oriented philosophy would probably result in a program which not only emphasizes strictly individual and dual sports but also has potential team sports, such as swimming, conducted event by event on an individual basis. The organization-minded director, on the other hand, probably would try to foster the group aspects of swimming and have swimmers earn points toward a team total.

It must be remembered that the director does not make program decisions without due regard for the wishes of the participants. Student interest must be sought, because it is the fundamental purpose of an intramural program. As much as possible, and as long as it makes sense, students should be permitted to play what they want to play. However, students should understand that when conflict arises, they should probably defer to a higher authority. The director of intramurals must have the final say in program matters. It is he, after all, who has the professional training with which to make decisions in intramurals.

A typical conflict of interest that occurs between director and students involves the appropriateness of including in the intramural program sports that are generally considered to be rough and dangerous. In those cases, in which safety is the issue, the director should take a firm stand in favor of eliminating or severely modifying the sport in question.

For a sport to be successful in the intramural program, there must be a sound foundation for its inclusion. Students will not participate in an activity to any significant degree unless they have had previous exposure to it, either as participants or spectators. The common sports of football, basketball, softball, golf, and tennis are no problem; but activities like fencing or gymnastics require some sort of preliminary instruction such as a physical education class, sports club, or clinic.

In some schools, certain parts of the intramural program are direct outgrowths of physical education classes. The gymnastics teacher, for instance, might request the intramural director to include a gymnastics meet in the program so that students in gym classes can have a chance to perform under competitive conditions.

Clinics seem to be the best way to introduce games which require little instruction but need explanation. Angle ball is a good example of such a game. Clinics can also be conducted to improve the play of moderately known activities such as badminton and volleyball.

Area interests, geographical location, and climate combine to affect program offerings. Lacrosse can be found in the Maryland, Virginia, and New York areas. Surfing is available at institutions along the southern coastline. Winter sports such as ice hockey, skiing, and speed skating are prominent in the northern and high-altitude sections of the country. Riflery, archery, and bait casting contests are held at institutions located in hunting and fishing areas.

Climate not only affects what is offered but also when sports are conducted. Outdoor activities such as golf, softball, and tennis are difficult to schedule in areas where the weather is particularly rainy or cold during most of the school year.

The school calendar itself can dictate what and when activities are conducted. Many schools begin classes in early September and end in late May; others start in late August and conclude in the middle of May. Still others start in late September and end in early June. The type of calendar system (quarter or semester) can affect sports programs. An institution in the north that ends its school year in mid-May would have difficulty in scheduling softball when cold weather persists into April. Lengthy golf and tennis tournaments in the spring would also be affected.

The nature of the student body and school have much to do with intramurals programming. At the larger institutions, where student bodies are normally residential, there are few problems in offering and scheduling desired activities because the students are close by and readily available during the course of the day. Commuter-based schools, however, pose special problems in scheduling and, in turn, in arriving at a program of activities. Because of their mobility and probable interest in off-campus activities (full-time jobs, perhaps), commuter students are difficult to draw back to the campus for school-sponsored programs. The intramural director must use his imagination in devising quality tournaments that stimulate student interest.

Because nonresidential students are frequently unavailable for dual and team sports, program emphasis should probably lean toward individual events conducted in a meet or short-term form. Somewhere along the line, lengthy tournaments usually produce conflicts with other student activities, and forfeits result. Wichita State University provides a good example of an institution which has a student body comprised mostly of commuters.

Wichita State University is located in Wichita, Kansas, population 280,000. The student body at the university numbers 14,000; about 90 per cent of the students live off campus and approximately 80 per cent have full- or part-time jobs. The vast majority of students, therefore, have little time beyond that which is necessary for attending classes, doing homework, and holding down jobs. In addition, any scheduling of dual or team sports becomes a problem because teammates have difficulty in coordinating free time among themselves, let alone with a fixed intramural schedule. Therefore, the program of activities at Wichita State has been established to suit the interests and availability of the students at large.

Because Wichita is a basketball town, intramural basketball survives on its own merits, but other team sports such as football and softball present problems. The large numbers of required players per team makes participation difficult for most people on campus. To meet that problem, touch football was modified so that only six players constitute a team, and consequently, participation increased.

The emphasis of the WSU program is on individual activities, which are held on a short-term or loosely scheduled basis. Cross-country, bicycling, and gymnastics are examples of individual sports held in one-day meets, Swimming, track and field, and wrestling could be considered as team sports, but are conducted as individual contests by event or weight class. The table tennis tournament, both singles and doubles, is run in one day. Weekends are used in scheduling two-day golf tournaments, and tennis is scheduled in a manner that allows opponents to arrange their own matches by deadline dates. Essentially, dual and team activities and lengthy tournaments are minimized.

The size of the institution and student body have significant effects on activity programming. Tournaments at larger institutions are likely to draw large numbers of entries, which probably result in lengthy schedules. Staffing is important in these situations. Directors of intramurals who have little supervisory help cannot easily conduct simultaneous tournaments. Their programs, then, are essentially limited to those events which can be run progressively throughout the year. However, the director who has a sufficient staff can easily conduct several tournaments at once and have all of them well supervised.

At smaller institutions, where intramurals is usually staffed by only the director, quality tournaments are very difficult to run simultaneously. Although contests usually must be scheduled one after another, problems usually do not occur, because the number of entries is generally manageable. Short tournaments in most events allow for the inclusion of a wide selection of activities. That situation, however, leads to a discussion of facilities.

Sports for which there are limited or no facilities cannot be offered. Golf tournaments cannot be scheduled where no course is available for play. Because the big schools tend to have better and more varied facilities than the smaller schools, it is more likely that one would find squash played at Penn State than at Bloomsburg State College in Pennsylvania. The more populous schools, then, may have greater potential for providing varied programs by virtue of their more extensive facilities.

The presence or absence of lighted outdoor facilities can seriously affect quality program offerings. Without lighted fields, large schools would have great difficulty in running touch football leagues unless large numbers of fields were available for play in the late afternoons; however, large numbers of games played simultaneously lead to problems in finding enough officials to man the fields.

The intramural budget has much to do with program scheduling. The purchase of necessary equipment and the hiring of officials and student supervisory help are particularly affected. Programs cannot be run without appropriate equipment and manpower, and the expertise of the intramural staff becomes important. Sports should not be selected for inclusion in a program unless there is someone on the staff who is sufficiently familiar with them to run the tournaments well. By the same token, good officials must be available for those sports that need officiating. Qualified people are sometimes hard to find for soccer, wrestling, gymnastics, and volleyball. The absence of capable officiating for a particular sport could be a significant factor in its omission from a program.

MODIFICATIONS

Almost any activity for which there is student interest can be included in an intramural program. Certain modifications are often necessary, though, for a sport to be popular or to be administratively sound in a given situation. Adjustments can be made in timing regulations, the number of players on a team, the size and nature of the playing area, the size and shape of equipment and goals, and in the rules themselves.

The most useful modifications are probably those regarding timing of contests. Because more than one contest is usually played per court or field per day, the length of a typical contest is important for scheduling and administration. Predictable contest length is one of the requirements for a smooth operation. Correspondingly, certain rules changes are often made to allow for more continuous game action within the particular time limitations.

The nature and skill level of the student body usually lead to modifications in the number of players on a team, which, in turn, leads to adjustments in the rules and playing area design.

While modifications are necessary to accommodate particular situations, it must be remembered that sports are usually most fun when the official rules are used. Modifications should be employed sparingly so that the "sense" of a game is not altered.

Examples of rules modifications follow.

Football

Of all the sports, football is the one that requires the most modification for acceptance into the intramural program. The tackling aspect of football must, of course, be eliminated and replaced by either a touch or a grabbing of a flag which is attached to the ball carrier's belt. Blocking, too, must be either modified or eliminated entirely.

The relative merits of flag and touch football essentially rest with the question of which is the rougher game. Although there is room for argument, it would seem that fewer bumps and bruises result from touch rather than flag football. Vigorous efforts are often required to wrest a flag away from a ball carrier who is actively protecting it. Body contact is therefore more prevalent with the flag game. Of course, touch football can be made rough by forceful tagging, but that can be effectively controlled through good officiating and the issuance of roughness penalties.

Flag football does have one distinct advantage over touch in that an official's judgment on the legal "tackle" is virtually removed. Either an opponent has obtained a runner's flag, or he hasn't. Legal touches are subject to far more uncertainty and, therefore, more potential error on the part of the official. This advantage of flag football, however, does not appear to justify the potential added roughness. Besides, the playing of touch football makes the procurement, maintenance, replacement, and guarding of flag equipment unnecessary.

Blocking is the aspect of touch football which requires the closest attention. There really is no completely satisfying blocking rule short of eliminating it altogether. The problem rests with the judgment and interpretation that must be made by the officials. If the rule is so modified that it permits only checking by the body, officials must be very alert and consistent in order to prevent the wholesale violations that very often occur from both sides of the lines. It is so very easy and tempting for linemen to illegally throw elbows at one another that an early and strict adherence to the rules must be enforced to avoid an escalation in roughness. It is difficult, though, to find many officials who are capable of such action.

On the other hand, a more physical block could be allowed, in which the only restriction beyond regular football rules is that the blocker cannot leave his feet to make the block. This is an easier rule on which to make an official judgment, but it also increases the incidence of injury.

Two examples of football rules follow:

PENN STATE UNIVERSITY TOUCH FOOTBALL RULES

The intramural department is not responsible for any injury or accident that may occur during intramural activities. Students are urged to obtain student accident insurance.

1. TEAM

Nine (9) players constitute a team. For plays that start from scrimmage, both offensive and defensive teams may line up in any manner they choose *except* that no offensive player shall line up within two yards of a sideline or lie on the ground to conceal his position.

2. FIELD

The playing field shall be 80 yards long and 40 yards wide. There shall be a 10-yard end zone at each end of the field. Goal posts will be placed on the back line of the end zone. The field shall be marked by lines dividing the field into four 20-yard zones. The inbounds line shall be 10 yards in from the sidelines.

3. TIME

The game shall be played in halves of 20 minutes each. The rest period between halves shall be 5 minutes. Each captain may call one time out (2 min.) each half. Game watch will be stopped during called time-outs, after each score, and during penalty discussions. It will also be stopped when it becomes apparent that play will be delayed because of unusual circumstances (injuries, etc.).

Watch will be stopped after *each play* during the last 30 seconds of both halves. During these periods the offensive team will still be required to put the ball in play within 30 seconds from the time the official spots the ball and marks it ready for play. If play involves a kick (field goal or punt) clock will start with kick—not snap from center, although the ball must be kicked within 30 seconds from time it was marked ready for play.

4. START OF GAME

The team captain winning coin toss may elect one of the following: kick, receive, or goal to defend during first half. At the start of the second half the teams will reverse field positions, and the team that kicked-off at start of game will receive.

5. KICKOFF

The kick-off shall be made from the kicking team's 20-yard line. It must be a place kick, and the ball cannot be teed up in any manner. The receiving team *must* position *five* men on the midfield line (restraining line). The kick must travel 20 yards before becoming a free ball. If ball goes out of bounds (before being touched) on kick-off, it shall be put in play by the receiving team on the midfield line, or at point where it went out of bounds if it travels less than 20 yards.

6. SCRIMMAGE PLAYS

Prior to each scrimmage play the offensive team *must* huddle within the inbounds lines. All players of the offensive team must participate in this huddle (see substitution rule).

Prior to start of play, offensive team must come to a "set" position for one second. *One player only* may be in motion providing he is not moving forward.

7. FIRST-DOWNS

A team shall be allowed four downs to advance the ball across each zone line (these are 20 yards apart). Each time a team advances the ball across a line it is awarded a first down (if play carries ball across more than one line it earns only *one* first down), and will be allowed four more downs to make the next zone line.

Upon a change of team possession, the line to gain shall be that line immediately downfield from the spot where the ball becomes dead. In case of penalties during play, the line to gain shall not be established until the penalties have been assessed.

8. TOUCH

One hand touch above the ball carrier's knee. Unnecessary roughness in making the touch shall be penalized.

9. BLOCKING AND CHARGING

The type blocking and charging common to regular football is strictly prohibited. This refers specifically to the shoulder and body blocks used to open holes in the line, or to clear a path for a runner on end sweeps and kick returns.

Legal Blocking

Offensive players may block on or behind the line of scrimmage only. No contact blocking is permitted beyond the line of scrimmage, or on kick returns. Blockers must keep both arms in contact with the body and may move into the path of a defensive player in order to impede his rush. The resulting contact must be light—it is intended only to slow down the rusher. Blocker cannot charge into an opponent.

Defensive Rushing

Defensive players are permitted to use their hands to ward off blockers, but violent shoving or pushing is prohibited. They must attempt to go around the offensive man.

It is the intent of the above rule to provide the offensive team with the means to protect the passer for a few seconds in order that he might pick out receivers. It *is not* designed to make possible running plays through the line, or end sweeps that require substantial body blocking in their execution.

10. PASSING

All forward passes must be thrown from a point behind the line of scrimmage. A team may throw more than one forward pass during a down *provided* that all such passes are thrown from behind the line of scrimmage. All players on the offensive team are eligible receivers. *Lateral passes only* are permitted beyond the line of scrimmage. Either team can recover a fumbled or incomplete lateral pass, but only the offensive team can advance such recovery (unless intercepted or recovered before ball strikes ground).

Restrictions on use of forward pass:
(A) No forward passing beyond the line of scrimmage. A pass thrown beyond this line is an illegal pass—penalty is 5 yards from spot thrown, plus loss of that down. An intercepted illegal forward pass belongs to the intercepting team.
(B) No forward passing on kick-off, punt, or other kick return.
(C) No forward passing following an interception.

11. FUMBLES

All fumbles may be recovered by either team, but only the offensive team may advance the ball following a recovery (unless the defense recovers in midair).

12. DEAD BALL

The ball shall become dead in the following situations:
(A) When the player in possession is legally touched (touch must be above the knee).
(B) When any part of the ball carrier's body other than hands and feet touch ground.
(C) Following an incomplete forward pass.
(D) Following recovery of a fumble by defensive team (unless recovery is made in midair).
(E) When ball goes out of bounds.

13. KICKING

When the offensive team elects to kick it must call the play "kick." Defensive team must have 5 men on the line of scrimmage. No player on either team may cross the line of scrimmage until the ball has been kicked. The kick must be made within the 30 seconds permitted to get ball in play. Fair catches are not permitted (see section on field goal attempts).

14. SCORING

Touchdown — 6 Points

Try after touchdown — 1 point (kick or run). If placement is to be attempted, it shall be made under same conditions as outlined below for field goal attempts.

Field Goal — 3 Points

Team must announce intention to attempt field goal. Neither offensive or defensive players may cross the scrimmage line until ball has been kicked. The kick must be made from a spot directly behind the point from which ball is centered. The ball shall not be teed up in any manner for placement attempts.

Defensive players are not permitted to get on the shoulders of a teammate, nor to employ the assistance of another player in hurdling to block placement attempts.

Note: When a field goal attempt falls short, and the ball remains in the field of play, it is treated as a punt. If the ball is blocked by the defense, and does not cross the line of scrimmage, it may be recovered and advanced by either team. However, if advanced by the kicking team the ball must cross their line to gain if they are to retain possession (if kick was made on fourth down). If kicking team does advance blocked attempt beyond their line to gain they will earn a first down and it should be recorded as such. If the ball is touched during the kick and goes beyond the line of scrimmage, the ball becomes free and can be recovered by either team, but can be advanced only by defensive team. A recovery in this case by the kicking team will give them possession, but not a recorded first down. If the ball falls into the end zone untouched, it is a dead ball.

Safety — 2 Points

Safety rule is same as that for regular football. When the offensive team is responsible for grounding the ball, or gets touched behind its own goal line, a safety results. *However,* the *impetus* that caused the ball to go across the goal line must be provided by the offensive team; otherwise it will be ruled a touchback. Following a safety the offensive team shall put the ball in play by a *place kick* from its own 20-yard line, with all the provisions of a kick-off in effect.

15. SUBSTITUTIONS

Unlimited substitution permitted under following conditions:

defensive team—substitution anytime ball is dead.

offensive team—substitutions must be made before team breaks huddle, and all incoming players must participate in huddle. (The purpose of this procedure is to eliminate undesirable tactics that have been devised to set up sleeper plays by employing tricky and confusing substitution maneuvers.)

16. EQUIPMENT

Spiked or cleated shoes are prohibited. Players may not wear any device that might cause injury to other players.

17. TIE GAMES

If teams are tied in score, the team with the most *first downs* will be declared the winner.

If teams are tied in score and first downs, an overtime series of plays will be run. The ball shall be placed on the midfield line, and one team will start a series of four downs (choice of first offensive series by toss of coin). Team *A* (offense) will attempt to advance ball as far as possible into *B*'s territory in four consecutive downs. Team *B* will then take over ball at point where *A*'s series ended. The position of the ball at the conclusion of *B*'s four downs will determine winner—if ball is in *A*'s territory then *B* is the winner. The game will end immediately when the team having the last offensive series advances the ball into opponents' territory—it will not be necessary for them to complete any downs remaining in their series.

If a team scores a touchdown in the overtime series, it shall attempt the extra point (not to count as a down); then the ball will be brought back to midfield and the same team will run any downs remaining of its four.

An interception or recovery of a fumble by opponents will terminate a team's series of downs. The recovering team will start play from the point where the recovery was made, or where the interception run-back ends.

No punting or field goal attempts are permitted in the overtime series.

Additional overtime series will be run if necessary. Team that ran first offensive series in the initial overtime will also start subsequent series on offense. In all overtime series, teams will defend the same goals they had during second half of game.

18. PENALTIES

Off-side—5 yards

Illegal motion—5 yards

Intentionally grounding ball—Loss of down and 5 yards from spot of pass

Illegal forward pass—Loss of down and 5 yards from spot of pass

Illegal procedure—Loss of down
  no huddle
  too many players on field
  offensive player within 2 yards of sideline
  delay of game
Unnecessary roughness*—15 yards (may also result in disqualification of player)
Unsportsmanlike conduct*—15 yards (may also result in disqualification of player)
Defensive pass interference—offensive team ball at point of foul—automatic first down (will be recorded)
Offensive pass interference—15 yards and loss of down

19. PROTESTS

Only those protests involving questions of player eligibility will be considered by the intramural office. These must be submitted in writing at the I.M. office within 24 hours following the contest in question.

Questions that arise on the field of play concerning rules and interpretations, officiating procedures, etc., will be decided immediately by the intramurals supervisor on duty at the play area. The decisions of the supervisor will be final.

> *Important:* **If team captain believes officials have erred, he should request that an officials time-out be called and the I.M. supervisor consulted before play continues.**

TOUCH FOOTBALL RULES

1. TEAM

Five (5) players constitute a team.

2. FIELD

The playing field is 50 yards long and 25 yards wide. There are 10-yard end zones and a midfield line.

3. TIME

There are two halves of 18 minutes each. Half-time period is five minutes. Two times out per game are allowed each team. Times out last two minutes each. Game watch runs continuously except for times out, after scores, during penalty discussions,

---

*Referees have been instructed to disqualify players who persist in rough and dangerous play. It must be borne in mind, however, that the players themselves ultimately determine whether or not play in a game becomes rough. Individuals who desire heavy contact should report to the varsity football squad.

and in the case of an unusual delay. The watch also is stopped after *each play* during the last 30 seconds of both halves. The offensive team has 30 seconds in which to put the ball in play after the official marks it ready.

4. START OF GAME

There is no kick-off. Ball is placed on midfield line for first series of downs. Captain winning toss of coin has choice of taking the ball, playing defense, or goal to defend. At the start of the second half, field positions are reversed and the team that initially played defense plays offense. Play is again begun at the midfield line.

5. SCRIMMAGE PLAYS

Prior to each scrimmage play, the offensive team must huddle. All players of the offensive team must participate in this huddle. Prior to the snap of the ball, all offensive players must come to a "set" position for one second. *No* men are allowed to be in motion.

The defense may rush the quarterback after a count of three, which is made and signaled by the official.

A team has four downs in which to score a touchdown. There are no first downs, punts, or field goals. Ball may be advanced by passing or running.

6. PASSING

All forward passes must be thrown from a point behind the line of scrimmage. A team may throw more than one forward pass during a down, provided that all such passes are thrown from behind the line of scrimmage. All players on the offensive team are eligible receivers. Only lateral passes are permitted beyond the line of scrimmage. Either team can recover a fumbled or incomplete pass, but only the offensive team can advance such recovery unless intercepted before ball touches the gound.

7. TOUCH

One-hand touch above the ball carrier's knee. Unnecessary roughness in making the touch is penalized.

8. BLOCKING

THERE IS NONE. PERIOD! Any obvious attempt at blocking is penalized. Likewise, defenders may not interfere with an offensive player's progress in going out for a pass.

9. FUMBLES

All fumbles may be recovered by either team, but only the offensive team may advance the ball (unless the defense recovers in midair). It is *not* a fumble when, in making a touch, the defender knocks the ball out of the ball-carrier's hand. This is the case even when the defender only touches the ball in making the touch. The ball is considered to be part of the ball carrier.

Basketball

Basketball is a game which can be left essentially untouched. Usual modifications involve timing and the shooting of fouls.

BASKETBALL RULES

1. TIME

Game consists of two 16-minute halves. Five minutes are allowed between halves. Two times out (one minute each) per game are permitted.

Game watch is not stopped for foul shots, jump balls, out-of-bounds, etc. Only during the last minute of the game does the clock stop in dead ball situations.

Officials are instructed to stop the clock and issue technical fouls to those teams that attempt to consume time through obvious stalling tactics.

2. FOUL SHOTS

There are no "one and one" foul situations. Only two-shot and technical fouls are shot. For all other fouls the ball is taken out of bounds by the team fouled, and the player committing the foul is charged with a personal.

> *Exception: During the last two minutes of the game, and in any subsequent overtime periods, all fouls are shot and are* **two-shot** *fouls (except technicals).*

3. SUBSTITUTIONS

Subs may enter game any time ball is dead. However, substitutes must report to the timer and wait for the floor officials to grant entry. A technical foul is charged for failure to comply.

4. TIE GAMES

Overtime periods are two minutes. If the score remains tied, a sudden-death overtime period is played. The first team to score a point wins. During the last minute of the overtime period the clock is stopped in dead-ball situations. *All fouls are shot and are two-shot fouls* (except technicals).

Soccer

Soccer is a difficult game to promote for intramurals because of the number of men required to field a team and the infrequency of scoring.

SOCCER RULES*

1. A team shall consist of 5 players. One player will be designated as goalie and will wear a colored shirt to indicate his position. This player *only* will be permitted to use his hands to play the ball within the "penalty" area.

2. The goals and field are about the same as for girls' field hockey.

3. Game will be played in halves of 12 minutes each. There shall be a 5-minute rest period between halves. *No times out are permitted in soccer.*

4. Substitutions, including goalie changes, must be made when ball is dead. Players may not switch positions with goalie while ball is in play.

5. *Players must wear sneakers or a soft gym shoe. Players may also wear the soft shoe with molded cleats. No hard shoes of any type permitted.*

6. All the rules of regular soccer apply except as may be modified in the following:

   a. There shall be no off-sides.

   b. After an out-of-bounds the ball shall be put in play by a kick. Defensive players must be five yards from ball on an out-of-bounds kick-in.

   c. *The goalie only will be permitted use of hands to play ball within the penalty area. He may catch the ball and take three steps before putting the ball back in play by means of either a kick or throw. Opponents are not permitted to charge into the goalie when he has possession of the ball.* (Note: defensive players other than the goalie may play in the penalty area, but are not permitted use of hands.)

7. SCORING

A record of goals and corner kicks will be kept. If teams are tied in goals at end of game, the team with the greater number of corner kicks shall be the winner. If tied in corner kicks, a 5-minute overtime shall be played. If necessary, a second and "sudden-death" overtime shall be started, the winner to be the team scoring the first goal *or* corner kick.

---

*Developed by C. M. "Dutch" Sykes, Penn State University.

8. DEFINITIONS

Corner Kick

Awarded when a defensive player causes the ball to go out of bounds across his own goal line. Opposing team puts ball in play by a kick from the corner of field nearest point where ball went out of bounds. Last man to touch the ball before it goes out of bounds is considered to be the one who caused it to go out. A corner kick is a "direct kick."

Direct Free Kick

Awarded when opponents are guilty of tripping, charging, handling the ball, pushing, kicking, or jumping. A goal may be scored directly by the kicker.

Indirect Free Kick

Awarded on all out-of-bounds except corner kicks, and when opponents are guilty of unsportsmanlike conduct, dangerous play, delaying game, and too many steps by goalie when he has possession of ball. The kicker may not score a goal directly. That is, the ball must touch another player before going into the goal.

For all direct and indirect kicks, defensive players must be at least 5 yards from ball (or on the goal line if kick is to be made from a point less than 5 yards from goal).

Softball

Softball is usually played as either fast pitch or slow pitch. There are disadvantages to both. The nature of fast pitch is such that a very good pitcher can easily dominate the game. In addition, fast pitch games usually take longer to play per batter than slow pitch games. Slow pitch is a game with more consistent action and it is more fun for inexperienced players. The game is aggravating, though, to good players because they must drastically alter their swings in order to hit the ball.

If slow pitch is thought to be the more desirable game of the two, then an even better game is one, two, or three pitch softball. Here, the batting team provides its own pitcher and he tries to "serve" the ball to the batters. The rules stipulate that the batter has the opportunity to hit only one, two, or three pitches. In one pitch, for example, the batter must swing at the first pitch offered. The batter is out if he swings and misses, hits a foul ball, or doesn't swing at all. The team in the field supplies a fielding pitcher and the actual pitcher is not allowed to touch a batted ball. The advantage of this game over slow pitch is that the batter can take a normal swing at the ball.

Meets

Swimming and track meets can be modified to the extent that certain events are eliminated and the participation of individuals is limited to a certain number of events to prevent the dominance of a meet by a few.

Water Polo

Water polo is such a strenuous game that it must be modified to comply with the skill and endurance of the average swimmer. It can be played in shallow water where the participants are touching bottom or it can be played with innertubes.

Co-ed

Modifications for co-ed activities must be made with the female in mind. Potential roughness and male dominance should be minimized.

In volleyball, the standard rule is that a girl must hit the ball at least once before it can be returned to the other side.

Football can be played with the quarterback being a girl and the rule that any pass down field must be made by a girl. Blocking is severely reduced or eliminated.

Angle Ball

Angle ball is a game invented by Charles A. (Rip) Engle, former football coach at Penn State University. The rules of the game are presented in full.

ANGLE BALL RULES*

Angle Ball is played by two teams of 12 players each. The purpose of the offensive team is to dislodge their "goal ball" with the ball in play. The defense naturally attempts to prevent this. One point is awarded for each score. After a goal is scored, the scoring team must see that its goal is cocked.

Exceptions occur when the goal is tampered with. A score is disallowed if the offense interferes with the goal. A point is awarded (even if the ball is not dislodged) if the defense interferes with the goal while offense is attempting to score.

PLAYING REGULATIONS

Sec. 1. Two 15-minute halves, separated by a 10-minute rest period, constitute a game. Each team is permitted four two-minute times out per half.

Sec. 2. The visiting team shall have choice of goals in the first half. The teams exchange goals in the second half.

Sec. 3. Each half is started by a jump ball at midfield between a member of each team. Each team remains in its own end of the field (the half farthest from the goal they are attacking) until the ball has been tapped. Players jumping face their own goal.

Sec. 4. Players may run with the ball, pass it, or strike it with hands open or closed. The penalty for kicking the ball intentionally is one lap and the ball goes to the opposing team at the point of the foul.

Sec. 5. A ball-carrier may carry the ball in any direction. If, however, he is touched or tagged by an opponent, he cannot (at this time) throw for a goal or continue with the ball, but must pass the ball before taking three steps. The penalty for throwing at the goal or advancing beyond three steps is loss of possession. The ball goes to the opposing team at the point of infraction.

A tag is not a push or a stiff arm. Depending on the violation, the official can call an unnecessary roughness penalty. If the throwing arm of the offensive player is in forward motion at the time of the tag, the throw is considered a legal attempt to score.

Sec. 6. If it is advantageous to the defender, he may tie-up the ball-carrier rather than tag him. This must be done without leaving the feet and without charging or driving the opponent to the ground but by grasping the ball-carrier between his waist and shoulders. A legal tie-up results in a jump ball. The penalty for an illegal tie-up is that the ball goes to the offended team at the point of foul and a roughness penalty (laps) is applied to the offender.

Sec. 7. A free ball in the air is governed by the same rules which apply to pass interference in football. The penalty for violation is a lap and the ball is awarded to the offended team at the point of foul.

Sec. 8. The use of hands on opponents by members of the

---

*Rules courtesy of Rip Engle. Copyright © 1966 Rip Engle.

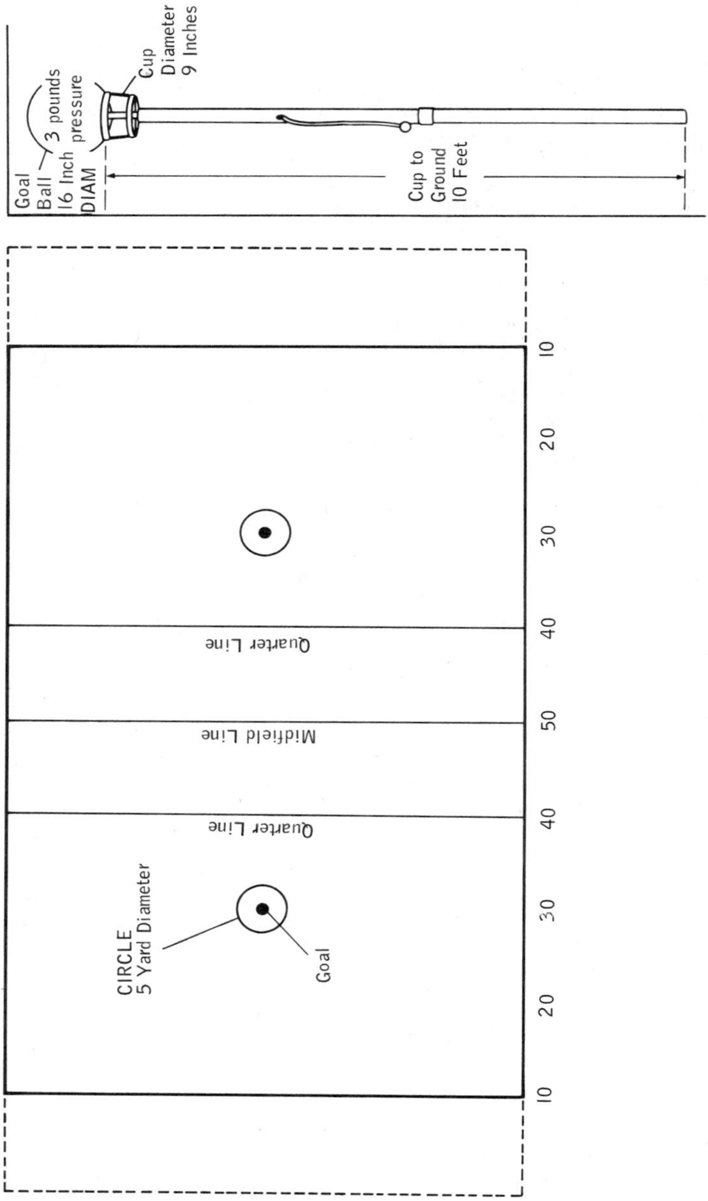

Goal
Ball
16 Inch
DIAM

3 pounds
pressure

Cup
Diameter
9 Inches

Cup to
Ground
10 Feet

10

20

30

40   Quarter Line

50   Midfield Line

40   Quarter Line

30

CIRCLE
5 Yard Diameter

Goal

20

10

offensive team is not permitted. For example, the ball carrier may not stiff-arm an opponent as in football. The penalty is a lap for the offender and possession to the offended team at the point of foul.

Sec. 9. The offensive team may screen for its ball-carrier with an upright screen but must not leave feet or use a shoulder block. The penalty is one lap and the ball goes to opposing team at point of foul.

Sec. 10. (A) Defensive team may use hands on the body of an opponent to ward off a screen. The defensive player using his hands to ward off an opponent may not use them to strike or stiff-arm an opponent.

(B) There shall be no unnecessary roughness such as tackling, use of hands about the head of an opponent, tripping an opponent, holding an opponent who is not in possession of the ball or charging an opponent before or after he passes the ball.

The penalty for any of the infractions in A or B is loss of ball at point of foul and one to three laps depending on the seriousness of the infraction.

Sec. 11. After a goal is scored, the team scored upon advances the ball to the quarter line (the line 30 feet from the scoring team's goal) without interference from the scoring team. Ten seconds are allowed to put the ball in play. The official need not handle the ball after a score.

Should the scoring team interfere with opponents with the intention of delaying the game the penalty is one lap for the offending player and the ball goes to the opposing team at the quarter line.

PENALTIES

Sec. 1. Fouls shall be penalized by giving the player at fault a prescribed number of laps to take around the playing area and by giving possession of the ball to the opposing team at the point of the foul.

Sec. 2. When the ball is awarded to the opposing team at an indicated point, all players must remain at least six feet away from the player putting the ball in play. Said player is permitted three seconds to put ball in play and must not take more than one step in doing so. Goal from here would not be allowed.

Sec. 3. In executing the penalty, the penalized player shall start at midfield on his team's side of the field and at no time enter onto the field of play until he has discharged the assigned penalty.

NOTE: Penalized player's team is one player short until he has taken his prescribed number of laps. He may return to the field or tag in a teammate.

OUT OF BOUNDS

Sec. 1. When the ball goes out or is carried out of bounds, an official shall award it to a nearby opponent of the player who caused it to go out. This player may carry or throw the ball in bounds and must do so within three seconds after being awarded the ball. If ball is carried in bounds, player must come in bounds at the point the ball has been awarded to him. If the player inbounding the ball fails to comply with these rules, the ball goes to the opponents.

Sec. 2. A player cannot throw for a goal while taking the ball in from out of bounds. If goal occurs, no score and ball goes to opponent.

Sec. 3. The 15-foot circle around each goal is out of bounds for players but not for the ball. The ball may roll through the circle and not be considered out of bounds. Such a ball may be tipped or passed by a player as long as he has not contacted the ground in the circle first (same as a sideline play).

SUBSTITUTIONS

Sec. 1. When time is out—(1) called time out, (2) jump ball, (3) out of bounds—any number of substitutes may enter the game.

Sec. 2. When time is in, a player on the field may be substituted for by going to his bench and tagging a teammate, who may enter the field of play at this time.

NOTE: If a team's times out are exhausted and a player is injured on the field, an officials time out should be called to remove the injured player.

General Information. Information on sports rules and the conduct of meets can be obtained by seeking out the coaches at the institution. Written rules and regulations for the conduct of meets are available through the NCAA and the National Federation of State High School Associations. Ordering instructions are included in all rule books published by both organizations.

Program
Regulations

If there is anything that can drive an intramural director up a wall it is his attempt to enforce program regulations equitably. For every rule that is established, there is always the occasional case for which the rule is unfair if imposed as written. The more rules in the program, the more frequently such instances occur. Although certain rules are unfair in specific instances, the absence of rules can also result in unfair practices. The director can save himself and participants a great deal of trouble by establishing only those regulations which are absolutely necessary for fair and orderly conduct of the program.

It is helpful to remember that an intramural program is not the NCAA, even though an emphasis on points, awards, and strenuous competition might make some programs seem so. The ideal atmosphere in which a program can be conducted is that of relaxed informality. The program is organized, but the organization is flexible enough to meet desired change; and the students trust the director to make fair judgments on specific situations and issues. The need for written rules is thereby minimized. Perhaps they could be replaced by written guidelines for intramural participation.

Written guidelines, rather than rules, seem to foster a more reasonable approach to establishing program order, because rules require enforcement, and fair enforcement is difficult in intramurals. An intramural director doesn't have the time to be a policing agent, so many inadvertent or purposeful violations go unanswered while a few are caught. The result is uneven and unfair administration, which could cause bad feelings among participants and toward the program. A more positive approach is to trust the students' sportsmanship and not actively look for violations. Player ineligibility is probably the most common program violation, and it is very difficult for the director to spot, anyway. Generally he must depend on the participants to report eligibility violations.

Program regulations vary widely from school to school, but most cover issues such as eligibility rules, conduct of participants, discipline, protests, postponements, and forfeits. The regulations used at Penn State University illustrate the finished product.

THE PENNSYLVANIA STATE UNIVERSITY INTRAMURAL DEPARTMENT

UNDERGRADUATE DIVISIONS

The following rules and procedures are intended to promote fair and orderly competition in the intramural program. These rules will be supplemented by additional regulations that will apply to specific sports in the program.

Section I—General Rules

A. There shall be three divisions for competition—dormitory, fraternity, and independent. Separate tournaments for each division will be offered in each sport, with championships being determined within each division.

Dormitory Division Only men living in university residence halls may compete in this division. An individual may play for or represent only the particular "house" in which he lives—Allegheny House may use only men living in Allegheny House, for example.

Fraternity Division Only bona fide members and pledges may represent a fraternity in intramural competition. An individual must be registered with the I.F.C. office as a member or pledge of a house to qualify under this rule. Unregistered "social" members cannot be used on fraternity teams.

Independent Division This division is intended primarily for men living off campus, but may include teams or individuals who cannot compete in either the dormitory or fraternity divisions. Teams composed of individuals from several dormitory units, or those having players from both dormitory and town areas on their rosters, must compete in the independent division. Individuals who desire to compete in sports of an individual nature, and who do not wish to represent any unit, may enter themselves in independent tournaments (tennis-singles, wrestling, etc.).

An individual may play for one team only in any sport. He is never permitted to play for a team in the independent division and also one in either the dormitory or fraternity divisions, nor can a player switch from one team to another during the course of a tournament. The *first* team that a player represents is the only team he is eligible to play with.

Individuals who move from one dorm unit to another, or who join a fraternity during the year, must finish a given sport season with his original unit. He may then represent his new unit in tournaments that start subsequent to his transfer. (Example: A man living in a dormitory plays basketball for the dorm team during the first semester, then pledges a fraternity. He must finish the basketball season with the dormitory team, but he can represent his fraternity in any sports that start after he officially becomes a pledge.

B. The intramural director may either waive or modify eligibility rules when it can be demonstrated that such rules would restrict the right of the individual to participate in an unreasonable or unfair manner.

C. The intramural director reserves the right to issue any new rules or regulations that he may deem essential to the success of the total program.

Section II — Eligibility

A. All male students registered as undergraduates (regular or special) shall be eligible to participate in intramural sports sponsored by the College of Health, Physical Education and Recreation, except as noted below:

1. Members of varsity and freshman sport squads may not compete in that particular I.M. sport, i.e., a basketball

squad member cannot play intramural basketball. The active squad rosters on the date of the first varsity contest in a sport shall be used to determine intramural eligibility. Any man who works out with a squad and/or retains his locker and squad equipment on or after the date of the first varsity contest shall be considered ineligible for the entire intramural season in that particular sport. If an individual wants to wrestle in intramurals, for example, he must drop from the wrestling squads before the first varsity wrestling match of the season. Drop dates are determined from records kept in the equipment room (the date the equipment and locker are turned in—not the date when the individual stops attending practice).

2. Varsity letter or award winners at this or any other four-year collegiate institution are ineligible to compete in the sport in which he won the award. The following are special applications of this rule:
    (a) Varsity letter winners and squad members in football cannot compete in I.M. touch football.
    (b) Varsity letter winners and squad members in cross-country are ineligible to compete in I.M. track events.
3. Any student receiving athletic grant-in-aid assistance shall be ineligible to compete in intramurals in the sport or sports responsible for such assistance.
4. Any student who has been declared a professional in a sport may not compete in that same sport in the intramural program.
5. In league or championship play-offs, teams cannot use players who have not played in at least one regular season contest for that team.
6. An individual who uses an assumed name, or plays under the name of another student, shall forfeit his right to participate further in the intramural program.
7. Teams guilty of repeated forfeitures in a tournament will not be permitted to enter subsequent tournaments.

B. A team shall forfeit any contest in which an ineligible player participated. Highly exceptional circumstances may justify some modification of this provision, but such instances will be rare.

Section III—Postponements, Forfeits and Protests

A. *Postponements.* No scheduled contest shall be postponed except with the consent of the intramural office. Postponements are rarely possible in team sports.
B. *Forfeits.* A contest shall be declared forfeited to the team or individual ready to play in cases where the opponent fails to appear within the established schedule time limit. For most sports this limit is 10 minutes after the scheduled starting time for the contest.
C. *Protests.* Only those protests involving questions concerning eligibility will be considered by the intramural office. They must be submitted in writing at the intramural office within 24 hours following the contest in question.

Questions that arise on the field of play concerning rules and interpretations, officiating procedures, etc., will be decided immediately by the intramural supervisor on duty at the play area. The decisions of the supervisor will be final. The unsupervised sports (tennis and golf) are excepted from this *no-protest* provision.

Section IV — Awards

A. Awards are given only to the champion in each sport. Present awards are as follows:

Dormitory	Each individual champion, or each contributing member of a championship team, shall receive a Penn State intramural medal. The dormitory unit shall receive a wall plaque trophy.
Fraternity	The organization winning a championship shall receive a trophy. No awards are made to individuals. In addition, the organization that earns the greatest number of points under the Fraternity Point Plan shall receive the E.C. Bischoff Trophy.
Independent	Individual champions, or each contributing member of a championship team, shall receive a Penn State intramural medal.

The type and number of awards is subject to change.

At some schools, a better approach to the eligibility of varsity lettermen might be to allow them to participate in their specific intramural sports only after a one-year absence from varsity competition. While eligibility rules are designed to equalize competition to some degree, they are not intended to prevent students from rightfully competing. A total ban on intramural basketball competition for a student who lettered as a freshman and then quit might seem unreasonable to some students. Since he no longer plays varsity, where is that student's outlet for competition if not intramurals?

Participants in an intramural program are expected to display appropriate sportsmanship with respect to conduct during contests and adherence to the spirit of program regulations. The competitive nature of the program often influences student behavior. The more competitive the program (points, awards), the more frequent occurrences of unsportsmanlike conduct are likely to be. When discipline is necessary, the usual procedure is to restrict the offender's future participation in the program either for that particular sport or for a specific length of time, such as a semester or year.

What makes the enforcement of rules difficult is the question of intent on the part of the offender. Was it intentional or unintentional? If unintentional, should the rule be enforced as stated? This is a common problem in intramurals. Experience is the best teacher of how to fairly write and apply the rules. It must be noted, however, that the purpose of intramurals is to encourage participation. Whenever there is doubt in decision making, it is usually proper to give the student the benefit of continued play.

Team rosters can aid in solving eligibility problems, but they are often not substantial sources of evidence, since names can easily be misrepresented. Those violations which are found through team rosters are usually those which are committed unintentionally, anyway. Rosters are further discussed in the section on program evaluation.

Almost all post-game protests can be eliminated by having a competent supervisor rule on problems as they occur on the field or court of play. Those which linger after the game is played should be settled quickly and fairly by the intramural staff. Again, an atmosphere in which the students trust the director and staff to make a judicious decision is best for intramurals. The "safer" procedure is to establish an intramural council which not only rules on protests but approves and initiates program changes. The size of the council must be workable, and is usually comprised of representatives from each organization, each group of organizations, or each classification of participants.

Forfeits are to be avoided like the plague because they can kill a program. Forfeits tend to snowball in a tournament when participants who appear for scheduled contests for which the opponents do not show subsequently forfeit future contests for lack of interest in winning merely by forfeit. It is very frustrating for students to appear for games, sometimes under trying circumstances (bad weather, exams), only to have the other team forfeit.

Aside from implementing point systems, several things can be done to reduce forfeits: (1) Do not take entries over the phone, and establish at least a token entry fee even if the money is not needed. It is important to separate the interested students from the more casual by making them put forth some money and effort in order to enter. Phone calls are too easily made by those who might later decide they are not really interested in playing. (2) In addition to, or in place of, an entry fee, establish a forfeit fee which is submitted at the time of entry and is returned after all schedule commitments have been met. Should an entry forfeit during the schedule, the fee is retained by the intramural office. (3) Do not allow groups or individuals who have forfeited an unacceptable number of past contests to enter subsequent ones. (4) After a team has forfeited a contest, call the captain and determine why his team forfeited and whether or not his team intends to meet the remainder of its schedule. Explain to him the adverse effects that forfeits have on the program. If he can no longer field a team, perhaps an interested team which missed the entry deadline would like to substitute into the schedule and assume the record of the team which has dropped out.

Policies on injuries and medical examinations are usually determined by the school administration. The director simply abides by, or improves upon, the regulations and carries out the established procedures.

Units of Competition and Point Systems

UNITS OF COMPETITION

Units of competition are organizations or student group-ings which classify participants for intramural play. At many schools, units are naturally formed as fraternities, sororities, dormitory units, departments, classes, homerooms, sections, or other established organizations. Unaffiliated students are placed in the independent category.

Established units of competition have a cohesive effect on intramural programming. The most successful units are those in which the students live together or, at least, have a common and frequent meeting place where announcements can be made, activities organized, practices scheduled, and strategies discussed.

Organization within the intramural program depends largely on the number and types of units. A large university might have separate divisions for dormitory, fraternity, sorority, co-ed, independent, graduate, and faculty groups. A smaller school might combine all undergraduate men as a unit, undergraduate women, graduate and faculty men, and so forth. In a large high school, homerooms or sections might compete on common grade levels. Small schools would have students of all grades competing against each other, with units formed by members of the same grade or by mixing units with students of all grades.

Urban colleges are a particular problem because of the large number of students who are unaligned with living quarters or organizations. Some programs try to form residential units by geographical location. These do not work well, though, because students within an area generally are not well organized and communication is difficult. One alternative is to establish academic departments, classes (e.g., freshman or sophomore), or clubs and organizations as units of competition. However, this system presents at least one problem. For a program to work well and fairly under a point system, the units of competition must be nearly equal in size. Large groups and those primarily composed of athletes or physical education majors possess an unfair advantage. Another alternative is simply to group all independent students into a single division and forget about a group point system. If a point system does seem desirable, one based on individual rather than group achievement may be used.

POINT SYSTEMS

Point systems are used in many programs to record an individual's or group's competitive progress throughout the year. Points are awarded for achievements in each activity and added for a yearly total. In that way, competitors vie for an all-year point award.

The applicability or desirability of a point system depends to a great extent on the institutional situation, but there are several basic purposes that should be examined.

Point systems provide a service to the students in allowing them to compare relative performances. It is interesting and stimulating for participants to compete on an all-around basis. Some directors, however, think of a point system as a device which artificially stimulates increased participation.

Typically, point systems in conjunction with all-year awards encourage rivalry among groups, lead to unethical practices in attaining points, and result in the common practice of placing group pressure on individuals to participate in contests in which they might not otherwise compete. Points and awards, rather than just the fun of playing, become the driving force behind participation. However, that is not the object of intramurals. Intramurals should be a voluntary, pressureless program.

Whether point systems and awards stimulate new participation is a debatable issue. It seems likely that the organizational structure and natural enthusiasm of groups such as dormitories and fraternities do more to stimulate participation than any artificial means. This is true for all but those groups which have enough athletic talent to contend for the all-year award. All-year awards tend to be controlled by a few groups because talent and good organization tend to perpetuate themselves. That is especially true in a fraternity division, where the active recruitment of athletes often takes place. The organizations which know very well that they have no chance at the all-year award probably enter tournaments for the fun of it or out of habit. Points or no points, significant numbers of students will participate in sports so long as the program is administered well and reasonable facilities, equipment, and officials are available.

Point systems are somewhat valuable for their positive effects on total participation and forfeits. Interested students participate as often as they can to gain points and to avoid losing points through forfeits. Especially in round robin tournaments, forfeits by teams who are out of the championship running are reduced because of the point penalty that would be imposed. Without a point system, one could expect a higher number of teams to forfeit remaining games when all chances at the championship are gone.

There are about as many point systems as there are intramural programs. Although systems must be adapted to particular situations, several considerations for developing a system can be identified.

Some organizations have significantly larger numbers of members than others. They must not be allowed to gain an advantage in compiling points simply because they have more participants. An organization must be limited to a specific number of teams and individuals in the various individual,

dual, and team activities. Specific limitations should probably vary with the number of entries that each unit can be expected to provide without putting anyone at a disadvantage. A standard rule is to allow each unit to enter one team in team sports, two teams in dual sports, and two or three individuals in individual sports. Anyone who does not represent the organization in competing for points may enter the independent division in which nonaligned individuals play and points are not a factor.

The key word for point systems is simplicity. Some systems involve so many categories for awarding points that they only lead to confusion and misunderstanding among participants, and they sometimes result in undue emphasis and concern with points. The effort required to tabulate a complicated system can be better directed to other aspects of the program. In addition, the best system is one which can be used for a variety of tournaments.

The emphasis of a point system should be on recognizing performance and the absence of forfeits rather than on entering and participating per se. In meets, points are assigned for place finishes and participation in all events for which an individual was scheduled. For other tournaments, points might be awarded for the winning of each contest, the winning of the championship, being the runner-up, and the completing of all scheduled contests without forfeiting. If bonus points for entering a tournament are part of the system, they must be assigned in conjunction with a no-forfeit provision; otherwise the program could be ruined. Teams or individuals who are not really interested in playing an activity could enter just for the entry points and forfeit all the scheduled contests. An intramural program is dedicated to serving only those who are sincerely interested in participating.

There are basic methods for handling forfeit points. Bonus points are either added to a unit's total for completing the schedule without a forfeit, or points are subtracted from a unit's earned total owing to the forfeiting of a scheduled contest. The better procedure is to add points rather than subtract them, because there is more chance of mathematical error with the latter, which entails addition and subtraction instead of just addition. Also, some units could end up with minus totals, which result in messy record-keeping.

Intramural activities have varied emphases within the program, so point assignments should vary accordingly. Point values could be categorized in descending order by team, dual, and individual sports. Further distinctions could be made on the basis of the typical number of entries per sport, the number of players required to form a team, and the repetitive nature of the tournament (round robin versus meets). If a sport (for example, tennis) is played twice during the year, the points for each tournament should be appropriately reduced to prevent undue emphasis.

Not every activity in an intramural program need be associated with the point system. Actually, there are disadvantages to having all sports played for points, especially at schools where the participation-to-facilities ratio allows an intramural program to include a large number of activities. Too many activities could overload the students to the point of having them play almost every day. In many units, there is a small nucleus of good, versatile athletes who want to, or are pressured to, participate in everything. In addition, certain sports are somewhat esoteric and potentially dangerous to inexperienced individuals who want to participate only for the points. Archery, fencing, riflery, and gymnastics are examples of activities which probably should be an outgrowth of physical education classes where the students can attain a sound basis for intramural participation.

Swimming, track and field, cross-country, and wrestling are also potentially dangerous sports, but many students are familiar enough with them to warrant inclusion in the point system. Caution must be taken by each participant to ensure that he is physically fit for the competition.

Three types of point systems are described and illustrated on the following pages.

Maximum-Minimum Point System

A scale is constructed whereby a maximum number of points can be earned by the tournament winner and a minimum number is assigned for the final place for which points are awarded. Normally, systems have more than one scale to accommodate differences between activities with regard to their importance or involvement. A team sport which is played in round robin fashion should rate a higher scale than an individual sport conducted in meet form, for instance. An arbitrary example of related scales is minor sports at 5–100, intermediate sports at 25–150, and major sports at 50–175. The assignment of points to those places which fall between the first and last is made by establishing point intervals between the places of finish. Intervals between places are a function of the maximum-minimum point spread divided by $P - 1$, where P is the number of places. For example, 20 places are desired in a tournament for which there is a 5–100 scale. The maximum-minimum point spread is 95, which is divided by $P - 1$, or 19, to arrive at an interval of five. The first-place entry would get 100 points, the second-place entry 95, the third-place entry 90, and so forth. Sometimes, the place intervals do not come out as whole numbers, in which case interval numbers must be rounded off.

A maximum-minimum system for six places might look like this:

Sport	Places—Points					
	1	2	3	4	5	6
Touch Football	175	150	125	100	75	50
Tennis—singles	100	81	62	43	24	5
Golf—medal	100	81	62	43	24	5
Handball—doubles	150	125	100	75	50	25
Soccer	175	150	125	100	75	50
Badminton—doubles	150	125	100	75	50	25
Cross-country	100	81	62	43	24	5

Maintaining a consistent number of point places throughout the intramural calendar makes for easy administration, because the point system can be established before the program begins. An alternative is to establish the number of places relative to the number of entries in the tournament. The number of places increases as the number of entries increases. However, all that can be established beforehand is the number of maximum and minimum points that each sport is worth.

The maximum-minimum point system is most applicable to tournaments which provide a clear ranking of entries such as meets, one-league round robins, or the Mueller-Anderson Playback. The nature of single elimination and double elimination requires the bunching of rankings, and certain participants must receive identical point totals. Also, the system cannot be used effectively for round robin play when more than one league is in operation.

Two important aspects of good point systems are missing with the maximum-minimum. The stability of a tournament is likely to be enhanced with the inclusion of no-forfeit bonus points. Some provision should also be made to recognize the difficulty of winning a tournament by awarding bonus points to champions and, perhaps, the runners-up. The point spread between the ninth and tenth place finishers should not be the same as the one between the first and second place teams. Greater significance should be placed upon a participant's advancement from second to first place than from tenth to ninth.

A Recommended Point System

Points are awarded in three categories: (1) points for completing a schedule without a forfeit; (2) points for each match or game victory; and (3) bonus points for champions and runners-up.

TEAM SPORTS: ONE TEAM PER ORGANIZATION

Tournament	No-Forfeit Bonus Points	Victory Points (per game)	Championship Points Champion	Runner-up
Touch Football	25	10	100	60
Basketball	25	10	100	60
Volleyball	25	10	100	60
Softball	25	10	100	60

DUAL SPORTS: TWO TEAMS PER ORGANIZATION
(per match)

Badminton	10	5	50	30
Tennis	10	5	50	30
Golf	10	5	50	30
Table Tennis	10	5	50	30

INDIVIDUAL SPORTS: THREE MEN PER ORGANIZATION

Tennis	5	5 per match	50	30
Badminton	5	5 per match	50	30
Table Tennis	5	5 per match	50	30
Wrestling	5	{ 5 per fall { 3 per decision	50	30

For meets, points are awarded by place ranking. Organizations may enter three men per event.

Tournament	No-Forfeit Bonus Points	Places									
		1	2	3	4	5	6	7	8	9	10
Cross-country	5	50	30	25	20	15	10	8	6	4	2
Cycling	5	50	30	25	20	15	10	8	6	4	2
Foul Shooting	5	50	30	25	20	15	10	8	6	4	2
Swimming											
50 yd free style	5	25	15	8	6	4					
50 yd back stroke	5	25	15	8	6	4					
50 yd breast stroke	5	25	15	8	6	4					
Track and Field											
100 yd dash	5	25	15	8	6	4					
440 yd dash	5	25	15	8	6	4					
mile run	5	25	15	8	6	4					
shot-put	5	25	15	8	6	4					

A team or individual must complete all schedule obligations in a tournament to earn bonus points for no-forfeits.

A player or team that fails to play at least one contest in a tournament shall receive no points for any victories that may have been attained by forfeit. This guards against the situation in which a team or individual wins the first match by forfeit then forfeits the remainder of the schedule.

Individual Point System

An individual point plan can be established in a manner similar to that for organizations. It is particularly useful at those institutions where a large group of independent students exists. The plan allows participants to compete in individual sports on an all-around basis. No participation in dual or team sports is included.

The individual who compiles the most total points from the eight individual sports will receive the all-year trophy for individual competition.

In all individual sports, the top 16 finishers will be ranked in order from 1 through 16. All-year trophy points are awarded as follows:

Place	1	2	3	4	5	6	7	8	9	10	11	12	13	14	15	16
Points	100	70	60	50	40	34	26	22	18	14	12	10	8	6	4	2

In the event of a tie, the points for the places in question will be added, divided, and appropriately assigned to the tied competitors.

Track and field and swimming operate in the following manner:

1. Each event has five place finishers.
2. Points are awarded as follows:

    1st   10
    2nd   8
    3rd   6
    4th   4
    5th   2

3. The overall 1 through 16 ranking for each sport is established by combining those points earned in all events.

The rankings for single and double elimination tournaments are as follows:

Places–Points

	1	2	3	4	5	6	7	8	9	10	11	12	13	14	15	16
Single elimination	100	70	55	55	30	30	30	30	9	9	9	9	9	9	9	9
Double elimination	100	70	60	50	36	36	24	24	13	13	13	13	8	8	8	8

Point Reports

Several times during the course of the year, point reports should be tabulated and distributed to all organizations and individuals involved.

It is helpful for participants to be informed of where they stand as the program progresses. A sample point report follows.

Unit	Badminton	Football	Tennis	Cross-country	Bowling	Basketball	Archery	Fencing	Horseshoes	Total	Place
Bradford	0	5	45	25	0	165	25	10	45	320	6
Oxford	30	115	75	20	0	95	15	0	0	350	3
Carbon	85	0	0	45	5	60	0	5	25	225	7
Brennan	10	75	40	45	15	85	25	30	15	340	4
Dunmore	20	80	65	0	0	20	35	40	75	335	5
Corbin	45	125	85	20	0	110	5	15	0	405	1
Benton	20	35	15	0	0	60	10	0	0	140	8
Stafford	35	95	50	35	10	75	40	25	30	395	2
Clinton	5	25	30	10	0	45	5	5	5	130	9
Douglass	0	15	10	0	0	35	15	0	0	75	10

Publicity and Recognition

PUBLICITY

Intramural publicity can take two basic tracks. Some directors believe that intramurals should be marketed and sold like any other product. The program is promoted through all sorts of printed materials, and participation is directly solicited through telephone calls to organizations that might otherwise miss, or have missed, the entry deadline. The practice is questionable from both the philosophical and practical points of view. Solicitation of entries often leads to the involvement of a number of only mildly interested participants who might eventually ruin the tournament by forfeiting. However, the real question is: who is intramurals for — the students who really want to play, or the director who is concerned with numbers? It is true that increased numbers often generate increases in funds and facilities, which is to the eventual benefit of the study body. But that is a potential reward; it doesn't do the current students much good. Besides, the whole idea of using the students for capital and monetary gain seems unpalatable.

A more sensible approach seems to be the use of publicity simply as a source of information for the community. What, when, where, and how to enter are the important items to advertise. In this manner the program sells itself through quality. Satisfied customers will come back for more, and new participants will be attracted by word of mouth or personal observation.

Intramural information can be promulgated in a number of ways, and no single method is likely to suffice for any one particular situation. Combined use of newspapers, posters, flyers, radio, handbooks, yearbooks, bulletin boards, and orientation presentations is necessary for effective publicity.

The most commonly used medium for publicity, especially for reaching organizations, is the intramural handbook. The size, format, and contents vary among schools, but the basic ingredients can be identified: calendar of events, regulations of the program (forfeits, protests, postponements, and so forth), entry procedure, injury policy, listing and location of facilities, schedule of free play times, and name, phone number, and office location of the intramural staff. The inclusion of additional items depends upon whether or not the program warrants it and the perceived purpose of the handbook.

Many handbooks contain philosophical messages from officials such as the president, dean of students, physical education department head, and the director of intramurals. Other common elements are the organizational chart of the department, history of the program, point system and awards, champions from previous years, organization and responsibilities of the intramural council, photographs of last year's champions, unit chairman's responsibilities, and records of participation. Some handbooks include sports rules, but this generally is not a good idea. Rules are better mimeographed for separate distribution; otherwise a whole handbook must be given to an individual who wants only the rules for one sport.

Unless a program is so well established that it rarely changes from year to year, a handbook-based publicity system can encounter one significant difficulty. In order to have the handbook ready for the next school year, all changes must be formulated and incorporated into the program so that the final copy can be presented to the printer three to four months in advance. The long-range planning that must be done in this situation eliminates the last-minute flexibility that is necessary when problems arise and changes are made.

In place of, or in conjunction with, an intramurals handbook, a system of information flyers (Figs. 1 and 2) may be employed. Prior to the entry period for each sport, flyers containing information on divisions of competition, entry procedure and deadline, nature of the game, time and place of contests, and type of tournament are distributed to established mailing addresses, intramural boxes, and to walk-in individuals who request them. At the beginning of the year, an introductory packet is distributed and serves as explanation of the procedural rules and regulations of the program (see Appendix A).

There are advantages to the use of the flyer system. For example, maximum flexibility is attained by printing materials within the intramural office. The initial packet can be formed and mimeographed shortly before use. Also, the advertising impact for individual sports is enhanced by a system which distributes information immediately prior to its intended effect.

For programs in which handbooks are the primary source of information, problems might arise if people forget to constantly refer to the intramurals calendar for entry dates. A supplementary system of flyers would act as an effective reminder.

Finances may be a factor in choosing between handbooks and flyers. Good handbooks cost hundreds of dollars to print. Flyers can be mimeographed quite cheaply. For their promotional value, however, handbooks may be worth the price. A handbook with pictures and an attractive cover is certainly nicer to look at than a stack of printed paper. The plus and minus features of each system must be considered in order to reach a balanced decision.

An outgrowth of the flyer system is the intramural newsletter, which can contain virtually any amount and type of intramural information. The newsletter is usually published weekly or monthly and publicizes upcoming events and meetings, results of past contests, current schedules, and

Wichita State University
Intramural Athletics

Frank Rokosz, Director
102 Henrion Gym

TABLE TENNIS SINGLES AND DOUBLES 1973

DIVISIONS

(1) undergraduate men (2) fraternity (3) undergraduate women (4) grad-faculty men (5) grad-faculty women (6) co-ed.

ENTRIES

Made at intramural office, 102 Henrion Gym. No phoned entries. Entry fee is $.25 per individual. Entry deadline is Wed., Oct. 3, 3:00 PM.

TIME AND PLACE

All matches are scheduled daily from 6:30 PM in Henrion Gym. The tournaments will be held from Mon., Oct. 15 to Fri., Oct. 19. Individual players and teams must be prepared to play more than one match per night. An attempt will be made to schedule singles and doubles play on alternating nights. Balls and some rackets are provided by the I.M. office. It is helpful for one to have his own racket.

TYPE TOURN.

Probably single elimination.

BASKETBALL 1973–74

DIVISIONS

(1) undergraduate men (2) fraternity (3) undergraduate women (4) grad-faculty men (5) grad-faculty women.

ENTRIES

Made at intramural office, 102 Henrion Gym. No phoned entries. Entry fee is $1.00 per team. Entry deadline is Wed., Oct. 10, 3:00 PM.

NATURE OF THE GAME

Game consists of two 16-minute halves. The clock does not stop in dead-ball situations except in the last minute of the game. All fouls are shot during the last two minutes of the game; otherwise, only two-shot fouls and technical fouls are shot. For all other fouls the ball is taken out of bounds by the team fouled.

TIME AND PLACE

Games are scheduled nightly (Mon.–Fri.) from 6:30 PM in Henrion Gym.

TYPE TOUR.

Round robin leagues.

Figure 1. Publicity Flyer.

other news of interest. The newsletter is particularly useful in programs which get little or no coverage in the school newspaper.

A concerted effort must be made to reach those students who are not affiliated with organizations that regularly receive intramural information. School and local newspapers seem to be the most effective outlet; almost everyone on campus picks up the school newspaper and scans it. However, it is essential that all intramural information appear consistently and prominently in a designated section of the paper. Much information can be missed by students who rely on the paper if intramural items appear only sporadically or are buried in some obscure section.

Independent students can also be reached through school or local radio stations and posters placed conspicuously

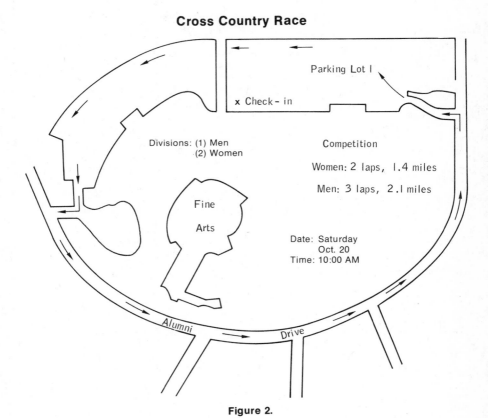

Cross Country Race

Parking Lot I

x Check-in

Divisions: (1) Men
　　　　　　(2) Women

Competition

Women: 2 laps, 1.4 miles

Men: 3 laps, 2.1 miles

Fine

Arts

Date: Saturday
　　　　Oct. 20
Time: 10:00 AM

Alumni　　Drive

Figure 2.

around campus. Posters depicting the intramural calendar (Fig. 3) are good for year-round use, and erasable posters can be used for advertising tournaments individually. To be an effective source of information, posters must be consistently maintained and kept up to date. They must also stand out among neighboring paraphernalia.

Most intramural programs have bulletin boards outside their offices. All types of intramural information can be posted

THE PENNSYLVANIA STATE UNIVERSITY
INTRAMURAL DEPARTMENT

Intramural Calendar—1971–72
UNDERGRADUATE DIVISIONS (Dormitory, Fraternity, Independent)
ENTRY DATES SHOWN ARE *FINAL*—LATE ENTRIES NOT ACCEPTED.
NO ENTRY BY PHONE

SPORT	TYPE TOURN.	ENTRY OPEN	ENTRY CLOSE	PLAY STARTS	APPROX. SEASON	SCHEDULE HOURS FOR TOURN. CONTESTS
Touch Football	Round Robin	Sept. 27	Sept. 30	Oct. 5	7 wks.	6:30 to 9:30 PM
Tennis—singles	Sing. Elim.	Sept. 27	Sept. 30	Oct. 5	6 wks.	*By arrangement with opponent
Golf—medal	Med. Pl. 36 Hole	Oct. 4	Oct. 7	Oct. 10 / Oct. 16	Frat. / Dorm.	Frat. Oct. 10 & 17 / Dorm. Oct. 16 & 17
Bowling	Round Robin	Oct. 4	Oct. 7	Oct. 14	14 wks.	6:30 to 8:30 or 9:00 to 11 PM
Basketball	Round Robin	Oct. 25	Oct. 28	Nov. 9	12 wks.	6:30 to 10 PM
Swimming	Sing. Elim.	Jan. 10	Jan. 13	Jan. 17	5 wks.	7–8 PM
Handball—singles	Sing. Elim.	Jan. 10	Jan. 13	Jan. 17	4 wks.	6:30 to 9 PM
Handball—doubles	Sing. Elim.	Jan. 31	Feb. 3	Feb. 8	4 wks.	6:30 to 9 PM
Wrestling	Sing. Elim.	Feb. 14	Feb. 17	Feb. 23	2 wks.	7:00 to 9:30 PM

Figure 3. Intramural Calendar. (*Continued on opposite page.*)

there, and the boards are particularly useful to students after office hours when no staff member is available for questioning. Some schools use bulletin boards as the primary source for intramural announcements.

Orientation programs might be conducted for new students. They can include anything from distributing packets of information at registration to a formal meeting and presentation of particular aspects of the intramurals program.

SPORT	TYPE TOURN.	ENTRY OPEN	ENTRY CLOSE	PLAY STARTS	APPROX. SEASON	SCHEDULE HOURS FOR TOURN. CONTESTS
Volleyball	Round Robin	Apr. 10	Apr. 13	Apr. 17	5 wks.	7:00 to 10 PM
Paddleball—singles	Sing. Elim.	Apr. 10	Apr. 13	Apr. 17	4 wks.	6:30 to 9 PM
Badminton	Sing. Elim.	Apr. 10	Apr. 13	Apr. 17	4 wks.	7:00 to 10 PM
Golf—team	Sing. Elim.	Apr. 17	Apr. 20	Apr. 24	5 wks.	*By arrangement with opponent
Tennis—doubles	Sing. Elim.	Apr. 17	Apr. 20	Apr. 24	5 wks.	*By arrangement with opponent
Soccer	Round Robin	Apr. 24	Apr. 27	May 1	5 wks.	6:30 to 9 PM
Horseshoes—doubles	Round Robin	May 8	May 11	May 15	2 wks.	6:30 to 8 PM
Track	Meet	May 22	May 25	May 30	3 days	6:30 to 8:30 PM

*In these tournaments opponents must contact each other and arrange to play by deadline dates established by I.M. dept.
FOR ALL OTHER TOURNAMENTS CONTESTS ARE SCHEDULED FOR SPE-CIFIC DATES AND HOURS. POSTPONEMENTS ARE IMPOSSIBLE FOR TEAM SPORT CONTESTS. SATURDAYS AND SUNDAYS WILL BE USED IN SCHEDULING *ONLY* IF ABSOLUTELY NECESSARY—OTHERWISE, SCHED-ULES WILL USE *MON. THRU FRIDAY* NIGHTS.
Notes:
1. Minimum player requirements   T. Football (9 men); Swimming (6 men); Bowling (5 men); Golf—team (5 men); Soccer (5 men); Volleyball (6 men).
2. Swimming events   50 yd. free style, 50 yd. back stroke, 50 yd. breast stroke, 100 yd. free style relay (4 men), diving.
3. Track events   100 yd. dash, 440 yd. dash, 880 yd. relay (4 men), high jump, long jump, shot-put (16 lb.).
ENTRY FOR ALL I.M. SPORTS MUST BE MADE AT ROOM 206 RECREATION BUILDING. *NO ENTRIES* ACCEPTED OVER THE PHONE.

RECOGNITION

An area closely related to publicity is recognition of achievement. There are several means of recognizing intramural attainments that also serve to publicize the program. Before mentioning specifics, however, a few thoughts should be given to one's philosophy and the interests of the participants.

Why do people participate in intramurals? Is it for the fun of playing, for the self-satisfaction it brings, for the prospect of an award, or a combination of these and other individual motivations? Desires vary among participants, but if a general assessment of goals can be determined, it must be juxtaposed with the ideal situation. Should the two differ, a decision must be made as to whether the general attitude of the student body is to be satisfied or whether the ideals of competition are to be imposed.

One has to believe, or hope, that the primary stimulus for intramural participation is something other than the attainment of an award. Most people probably get involved because intramurals, win or lose, is fun and recreational. In addition, there are no doubt motives of improving physical fitness and achieving social contacts. Personal pride might be a factor for others. Whatever one's goals, the pursuit of awards or points toward an award is one of the least desirable.

Especially in college, the emphasis of physical education is on lifetime sports. Educators stress the importance of physical activity throughout life as it relates to fitness and recreation. To maintain any form of judicious exercise in later years requires intrinsic stimuli. The opportunities for gaining extrinsic rewards are few and far between for most people. Those who are accustomed to participating in an atmosphere of structured competition and awards or other extrinsic rewards might have some difficulty in adjusting to the psychological requirements of self-directed action.

Another potential problem is the type of competition that tends to occur when points and awards are involved. Extrinsic stimuli sometimes lead to rough play and a lowering of desired sportsmanship standards; and in those sports that are self-officiated, participants may occasionally be tempted to call things their way unfairly.

It can be argued that the withholding of awards from an intramural program is unrealistic in light of the atmosphere in which youngsters typically grow. Extrinsic values tend to dominate young people's lives because educators (parents included) often reward appropriate behavior with a variety of "prizes." The prevalence of this philosophy of material compensation is far from ideal and can even be harmful. At some point, proper values must at least be communicated, if not actually learned. So the question is: Why can't the ideals and values of physical activity and sportsmanship be instilled in youth from the start? And why must there be a definite psychological transition between the school years and later life? Some people probably never do make the transition, and they gradually or suddenly become inactive. Surely, a certain number of those same people could have been properly stimulated to participate in unstructured activity throughout life.

Arguments aside, it does seem appropriate that champions be recognized in some fashion, even if only for the purpose of record keeping or substantiating the winning of an event as a news item. There are a number of means available for recognizing intramural achievement; the most common forms are trophies, plaques, medals, ribbons, certificates, school letters, and so forth. Description, cost, and purchase procedure for these items can be obtained through catalogs from companies which handle awards. However, for reasons discussed earlier, these are probably the least desirable forms of recognition.

If awards are to be employed in a program, several considerations require some attention. To whom are the awards to be distributed? In team sports, a team trophy or individual medals can be given to the champions only or to any number of place finishers. Trophies seem most appropriate for fraternities, dormitories, and other organizations that have permanent places in which to display them. Individual awards are more suited for loosely organized groups. A rotating trophy could be used for an all-year award, which is given to the organization that accumulates the most points in all sports under the point award plan. Typically, the trophy is permanently presented to an organization which wins it a prescribed number of times.

Awards should be engraved at least to the point of designating the particular sport and event, the divisions of competition, and the place finishes. If names and dates are desired, the availability of the awards will naturally be delayed until the specifics can be engraved after the event takes place. It is somewhat risky to have dates engraved on awards in advance of the actual activities. There are bound to be years when certain contests or divisions of competition are not held, in which case specifically engraved awards become useless for the following year.

The excitement of receiving an award is probably lessened if there is undue delay in presenting it. The most meaningful time to present awards is directly after an event is completed. However, this requires that the engraving be done in advance and no names be on the trophy. In some programs, the presentation of all awards is deferred to the end of the year, when a banquet or assembly is held. All champions are honored at that time.

Intramural awards should not be expensive. There is no need for symbols of recognition to have value in themselves. They are mementos, meaningful only to those who earned them. Besides, the more grandiose the award, the more dominant its influence is likely to be on the atmosphere and psychology of competition. Most programs can't afford to spend much money on awards, anyway. Awards are not a necessity, and the money could be better spent on other items that deserve more attention.

The most reasonable, justifiable, and meaningful symbols of intramural recognition are probably those which serve to publicize the program and the athlete simultaneously. Photographs or listings of all champions could be placed on a display board in a prominent area of the gym; they might also appear in an intramural handbook or school yearbook. Well written newspaper accounts are effective. All-star teams could be selected for team sports, and they serve to publicize those players who are skilled but are not on championship teams. Records of certain sports such as swimming and track and field could be publicized on display boards or in handbooks or yearbooks.

6

Officials

RECRUITMENT

Good officiating is a key to successful intramurals. An otherwise well organized program can fall apart on the field or court of play because of incompetent or uninterested officials. It is extremely important, therefore, that officials be sought who are genuinely interested in officiating and not in it just for the pay. Program effectiveness can be severely reduced by people who not only don't do a good job but only appear for work sporadically.

There are potentially good officials among the students at every institution. At some schools, sufficient numbers of new and veteran officials appear before the start of those sports which require them, and no advertising is needed. A good many intramural departments, however, must actively recruit the people they need. This might be done through newspaper and poster advertising, announcements, and personal contacts. Good pay, of course, is an important lure, but the best and most dependable officials usually turn out to be those who need no enticement and seek out the intramural office on their own.

It is wise to avoid the situation where officials for intramurals come out of an official's class as required laboratory work. Most class officials are not really interested in officiating intramurals. If they appear for work at all, it is usually because they want to fulfill their credit obligations; so the probability of their doing a good job is low. Use only those officials who volunteer for work.

One might imagine that the number of students interested in officiating and the competence that can be expected of them increase with higher pay. However, more pay and demands for greater ability do not always lead to better officiating. High pay will surely attract those who are interested only in money and not in conscientious performance. On the other hand, the director can probably weed out the worst officials without jeopardizing the program, because more officials are available at a higher pay rate.

If a good deal of money is available, the director might consider the hiring of a professional corps of officials for the popular team sports such as football and basketball. A number of beginning state-registered officials would probably be interested in steady work at a reasonable salary.

The matter of hiring professionals brings up the question of intramurals as education or recreation. If intramurals are viewed primarily as recreation, and sufficient funds are available, then every effort should be made to staff the program with professional people, including officials, secretaries, and assistants. A professional program is run by professionals. If education is a substantial goal, then students should be solicited for involvement in program administration. Graduate assistants, student supervisors, and student officials take significant responsibilities in running the program; this is usually the case in schools with limited finances.

TRAINING

Most officials who participate in the intramural program have had no officiating experience outside of intramurals. Therefore, some sort of training is required for both new and veteran officials before the start of each sport season. The type and degree of training depend on several interrelated factors.

If little money is available for payment of officials, and the officials are expected to go through an intensive training and learning of the rules, a director of intramurals might find himself with only a few students willing to work. If the pay must be low, and competence is still demanded, the director must resign himself to the probability that he will not have enough officials to cover every game day conveniently. Furthermore, it must be remembered that a certain surplus of officials is required for emergencies or on short notice.

One of the only ways to survive the high quality—low pay situation is to motivate the students to do a good job despite the pay. The director must almost babysit with the officials to convince them that their work can make or break the program. He should encourage them to study rules and mechanics on their own and perform self-analyses for improvement.

Although some programs require officials to take practical examinations and undergo courses of formal instruction, the most appropriate form of training is probably the one-night clinic. Rules are reviewed; field or court positions and areas of coverage are explained; the makings of a good official and his duties are emphasized; shirts and whistles are distributed; and procedures and policies of payment and scheduling are made clear.

The clinic takes place both in the classroom and on the gym floor. Supplementary to classroom instruction might be a demonstration of officiating techniques by veteran officials at an exhibition game. During the game, the clinic director should point out to the group the duties and proper positioning of each official and the techniques of making calls and handling the ball. It is a good idea to compile and distribute printed packets containing most of the material presented in the clinic so that officials can refer to the information during the course of the season. If funds allow, the director might also distribute rule books and officiating manuals obtained from the NCAA or National Federation of State High School Associations.

Beyond the initial clinic, there could be a midseason meeting of all officials for the purpose of reviewing common errors in technique and interpretation of the rules, as well as emphasizing good performances.

Although clinics serve a useful purpose, the most effective means of improving the performance of officials is to deal with them on an individual basis. Periodically during the season, the director should personally meet with each official and make suggestions for improvement. This may be done in a conference in the intramural office or, even better, during breaks in the play, such as half times and between games. Although criticism of performance is probably most effective when communicated shortly after game situations occur, the director must be careful to make his comments discreetly so the official is not embarrassed in front of those he is officiating.

Also, the director should be sympathetic to the officials and the conditions under which most officiate. It's not easy to work three or four games consecutively. When one is exhausted, there are bound to be occasional mistakes and mental lapses.

SCHEDULING

Programs that require a number of officials per day also require efficient scheduling procedures. Four good methods for scheduling officials are described.

Officials can be scheduled on a steady-day basis. A person who is given Monday and Wednesday, for instance, works those same days throughout the schedule. As illustrated below, a list of officials is compiled with phone numbers and steady days of work marked. A secondary list of alternate officials and phone numbers appears on the side of the sheet. They are not assigned days of work and are used as replacements for those who cannot appear on their regularly scheduled days. Standard policy is for officials to find their own substitutes and report the change one day in advance. Replacements may be either the listed alternates or other regulars on their off days. This type of arrangement seems most appropriate when a large number of officials must be scheduled per day.

Name	Phone	Mon.	Tues.	Wed.	Thurs.	Alternates	
Brown, J.	686-8987	X		X		Hendricks	687-8945
Miles, G.	686-4578	X			X	George	678-3269
Harvey, T.	678-2849		X	X	X	Hardin	687-5784
Jones, R.	686-4895		X			Kadel	789-5376

In conjunction with the list of officials, a total schedule of days for the season is also printed and distributed. Officials may then know when the season begins and ends and what days during the course of the season are blocked off for special events.

On any particular day, the day's list of scheduled officials is placed on an index card. The card is taken by the supervisor to the area of play and any changes or absences are noted on the card. The names on the card are later transferred to a master sheet from which the payroll is determined.

Officials could also be given steady days of work using a system that requires only one schedule. The game dates of the season are listed in order, and the assigned officials appear beside the appropriate dates. An alphabetical list of officials and their phone numbers also appears on the sheet to aid officials in contacting each other for the arrangement of substitutions. This system is most useful when only a small or moderate number of officials is needed per day.

Schedule	Officials	List of Officials	
Mon. Sept. 24	Jones, Smith, Rudi, Holbrook, May, Howard	Calvin	686-7986
		Holbrook	789-3748
Tues. Sept. 25	May, Smith, Calvin, Holbrook, Howard, Myslinski	Howard	789-4867
		Jones	787-2687
		Kahn	789-6247
Wed. Sept. 26	Smith, Calvin, Jones, Myslinski, Kahn, Ott	May	787-6785
		Myslinski	686-2468
		Ott	686-5743

Officials may be scheduled on a weekly basis. Every Monday during the season, the following week's complete list of scheduled officials is posted. Space to the right of each name is available for initialing. The officials who appear on the sheet have until Thursday to place their initials beside their names for those days on which they desire work. Blank lines are provided below each day's line-up so that officials who want to be alternates can print their names on the lines. In the event that some of the regularly scheduled officials have not initialed their names by Thursday, the director places an OK beside the names of the necessary alternates. It is the responsibility of all alternates to return on Friday to see whether or not they have been okayed for work.

Mon. Jan. 23	Tues. Jan. 24	Wed. Jan. 25	Thurs. Jan. 26
Jackson _____	Jurgenson _____	Haskell _____	Jones _____
Harvey _____	Kmietovich _____	Wilson _____	Johnson _____
Harold _____	Harvey _____	Jackson _____	Wilson _____
_____ _____	_____ _____	_____ _____	_____ _____
_____ _____	_____ _____	_____ _____	_____ _____
_____ _____	_____ _____	_____ _____	_____ _____

Instead of actually listing officials under each date, a number of blank lines equal to the number of officials required per day could be placed in each column. Officials get assignments by printing their names on the blank lines. The best officials are given first choice of days; the rest may sign up on a first come, first served basis. This system is most appropriate for programs in which a small number of officials is needed per day and the availability of officials cannot be determined on a steady day system.

Mon. Apr. 2	Tues. Apr. 3	Wed. Apr. 4	Thurs. Apr. 5
1. _____	1. _____	1. _____	1. _____
2. _____	2. _____	2. _____	2. _____
3. _____	3. _____	3. _____	3. _____
4. _____	4. _____	4. _____	4. _____

The seasonal and weekly styles of scheduling both have their advantages and disadvantages. The seasonal system is good in that the schedule needs to be formed only once. Officials are handed the printed schedule at the beginning of the season and need not make weekly trips to the intramural office to check a list. If all the officials adhere to the procedure rules for obtaining substitutes, the system works well. However, problems inevitably arise when officials have trouble finding replacements and notify the intramural office of that situation shortly before they are scheduled to appear for work. This puts an extra burden on the supervisor in charge. He must find another official or, perhaps, help officiate the games himself.

The chances of last-moment problems with officials changes are minimized with the weekly system. Here, officials can probably schedule themselves quite accurately, but they must be vigilant in checking the posted list on at least a weekly basis. Also, the director must take the time to draw up a new schedule sheet each week.

To some extent, discipline can be maintained among officials by manipulating their salaries. Each time an official fails to appear when scheduled, a certain amount of money is deducted from his total pay. In order to enforce this policy, officials are not paid until the end of each sport season.

REQUIRED OFFICIALS FOR EACH SPORT

The number of officials assigned for each game depends on the sport and how it is modified and the finances available. The usual method is to provide the minimum number of officials that can properly administer the game.

Basketball

Three officials are required per court. At any one time, two students officiate the game while one keeps score and time. Duties are rotated throughout the series of games for the day.

Football

Three officials are required per field. One official stands near the sideline and keeps score, operates the timer and first-down marker, and watches the play in the line. One official stands in the offensive backfield and one stands in the defensive backfield. Duties are rotated game by game.

Soccer

Two officials are required. While performing the regular officiating duties, one official is responsible for keeping time and the other keeps score.

Volleyball

One official stands on the sideline and calls the game as well as scores.

Softball

One or two officials are needed. There may be a plate umpire and a base umpire; or one umpire may control the whole game from behind the pitcher.

Starting a New
Program

As stated earlier, the intention of this book is to provide the reader with information that will allow him to organize intramural programs in a variety of situations. The flow of the book, however, leans rather heavily toward the collegiate situation. This is as it should be, perhaps, because one can then become familiar with the makings of highly involved programs and, from that, select appropriate elements for any number of limited conditions. Yet, something specific should probably be said about intramurals in the public schools since most students who read this book and take a college course in intramurals find themselves teaching in public school systems. Relatively few have the opportunity to assist or direct intramural programs on the college level.

While the focus of this particular discussion is on public school intramural programs, the information is applicable to other types of programs because as in public schools, they are usually small, one-man operations. Directors periodically come and go, and staff assistants are not available to continue the program. New directors must be appointed, and they may come from within or outside the current institutional staff. In either case, the new director is a new director, and he may very well be someone who has had no previous administrative experience with intramurals. It seems reasonable, then, to provide the reader with some specific information with which he can ease the pain and confusion of starting from scratch.

Just because one comes to an institution as a new director of intramurals does not necessarily mean that he must start *absolutely* from scratch. Some sort of program was probably in existence the previous year. The first step, then, is to investigate the old system. There may be records describing the activities and the statistics involved. Find them and read them. They will give clues toward the proper establishment of a program in that particular school. If records are unavailable, try to get information from the faculty and students. If no intramurals program existed in the past, you will simply have to begin without a tangible guide.

Don't flounder. There is a tendency to confuse oneself in the face of a completely new project by trying to think of too many things at once and not really getting anywhere. One must categorize things; ask oneself the right questions, know where to get the answers, and build the concept of the program by proceeding logically. Logical procedure does not necessarily imply a set sequence; however, certain elements of intramural organization and administration can be identified and must be dealt with. In fact, they are the very items of interest which have been discussed in preceding chapters, but the following summary may be helpful.

While there is no strict order for organizing the elements of administration, some must be considered before others. The order of presentation which follows seems logical in most instances.

1. Get to know who can be depended upon for information, and study the lines of responsibility (chain of command). Meet with the immediate supervisor and reach an understanding of the exact nature of the job, What are the responsibilities of the director of intramurals?

2. The major problem in establishing intramurals in the public schools involves three interrelated items — available facilities, scheduled use of facilities, and transportation for those who are bused to and from school. Varsity athletics typically occupy the facilities during the prime times directly after school. It is not at all likely that varsity athletics will move aside even occasionally, so intramurals must be worked around them.

Make a list of all the times that particular facilities are available during seasons of the year, during days of the week, and during hours of the day. Intramurals could be conducted on weekends, before school, during a typical break in the day's schedule, after school when varsity teams are not in session, or in the evening. In addition, some sports can be played out of season to avoid conflicts with varsity teams. For example, tennis and wrestling tournaments could be conducted in the fall and soccer and swimming in the spring. List the possibilities in order of preference, then make choices based on the practicalities of any given circumstance.

When intramural activity is scheduled during times other than regular school hours, some provision for transportation should be made for those who need it. This is usually a big problem, but it must be solved because good participation in the program probably depends on it. Investigate the possibilities with the school principal. If transportation cannot be provided, the resulting restriction in useful scheduling times will limit the scope of any intramural program.

3. Aside from facilities, determine the availability of other supplies. What is in the equipment room? What office supplies are available? Is there any money specifically budgeted for intramurals so that program assistants can be paid and needed items purchased?

4. Find out the legal liabilities involved in conducting an intramural program at the school. Use common sense to protect participants from dangerous situations. Pay particular attention to structures which protrude into or near the play area. Eliminate them, if possible. In any case, think safety, even at the risk of reducing the "fun" of a game or eliminating it entirely. Students often like to play games that have an element of danger in them, but few parents will accept that danger after one of their children is hurt playing under questionable circumstances.

5. Even though preventive measures are taken, some

injuries will occur during intramural play. Know the standard first-aid methods, and give some forethought to emergency procedures to follow in the instance of a serious accident.

6. Based on the many variables involved, develop a program of activities. The most popular sports are basketball, touch football, and softball, so work on those first. Although the program is likely to be dictated more by circumstances than anything else, be conscious of the need for soliciting the students' desires. Set up a student council or make an effort to talk to participants individually.

7. Determine the units of competition. Select units in which members are together frequently. Homerooms, sections, and classes (freshman, sophomore, and so forth) are logical choices. Independent competition can be established where units are not feasible. Teams for independent play can be organized in three basic ways: players can simply band together and form a team; a list of all interested students can be assembled and teams formed by random alignment of players; or captains can be named and teams formed by a drafting or pick-up process.

8. Formulate program regulations. They include eligibility regulations, modifications of sports rules, entry procedures, a point system, and guidelines on handling protests, postponements, and forfeits. A director's philosophy of intramurals comes in strongly when program regulations are formed. A philosophy of operation is difficult to envision at first, but it must be done even though it will probably change with time. Sit down and think things out clearly. There must be a good reason for anything done in intramurals, and it is important that program policies be consistent with program philosophy throughout. One of the quickest ways to get into trouble with students is to offer lame or inconsistent defenses for administrative procedures, or not to offer answers at all. Get things straight from the start. It requires a good deal of self-examination, but the time will be well spent.

9. Organize a system of communication between the intramural program and the students. Announcements are easily posted on bulletin boards or through the public address system. If the system used is one in which the students come to the announcements rather than the announcements going to the students, make sure that everyone knows where and when intramurals information is to appear. Consistency is important for student satisfaction and a smooth operation.

For instance, after entry deadlines pass, post or circulate the tournament schedules within a specified period of time. When participants look for information, they should be able to find it where it's supposed to be and at the expected time.

10. Develop a plan for recognizing intramural champions. Preference should be given to methods that serve to publicize the program.

11. Determine what kind of help is needed to run the program. Who will do the supervising, officiating, secretarial work, and field maintenance? These jobs might best be done by the director himself, but try to find competent assistance.

12. If possible, establish a calendar of events and publicize it. It's nice for everyone to know what the total program is likely to be.

13. Keep in mind the various sources of intramural ideas and of help in the structuring of contests. Use them.

14. It might be a good idea to make a list of things that must be done to conduct each type of tournament. Include the general items of publicity, entry procedure, structuring of the tournament, preparation of the facility and equipment, provision for officiating, and so forth. Under each general item make specific procedural comments. For example, under publicity one might want to list the following:

a. Two weeks before the entry deadline, formulate the necessary entry information and related contest descriptions.

b. Distribute announcements to the school paper, bulletin boards, and to established organizations one week in advance of the entry deadline.

c. Where appropriate, distribute information on the progress of the tournament.

d. At the end of each tournament, publicize the tournament champions.

All the talk about budgets, handbooks, and the like is nice, but what if there is no money for intramurals? The initial reaction might be to abandon the thought of organizing a substantial program. This need not be the case, however, because worthwhile activities can be conducted without special funds. As discussed earlier, intramural money is spent for the general items of equipment, supplies, and personnel. All the specific necessities for conducting an intramural program can be obtained without spending *intramural* money as long as the director is prepared to make a personal commitment.

Equipment should not be a limiting factor for playing the standard games of football, basketball, softball, volleyball, and so forth. Use the same balls and bats that are used for physical education classes. Colored jerseys are not really necessary for those sports that normally require them — go "skins" and shirts. Much of the special equipment which usually is employed in a well established program can be omitted. For instance, stop watches are not absolutely necessary for timing basketball and football games. Use a regular watch and play the game under continuously running time.

Office supplies should not be a real problem, either. Paper, typewriters, and mimeograph machines are usually available to faculty members. One of the regular secretaries might even be persuaded to do some occasional typing; that is all that is needed to develop publicity and records systems. The expense of awards is no problem — don't offer them at all. Use the school paper or the yearbook for recognition purposes.

Lack of money to hire personnel can have the most significant effect on the administration of the contests themselves. Competent officiating is difficult to obtain at any price, but with no money at all, it poses a real problem. Supervision must also be provided, but that should not be a serious problem, because the director can do it in most instances. Other faculty members can be asked to fill in when necessary. The officiating can be handled in two ways: the director does it himself, or volunteers are found among the faculty and students. Varsity athletes are a possible source.

What it all amounts to is that a program of sorts can be conducted under even the most trying circumstances. It must of necessity be less formal than those of endowed institutions, but the students will appreciate it and have fun nonetheless. And that *is* the name of the game, isn't it?

SECTION

II

TOURNAMENTS AND PROBLEM-SOLVING

Single Elimination
Tournament

CONSIDERATIONS

Single elimination requires the fewest number of contests to reach an acceptable champion. Participation is limited—one loss eliminates a contestant from the competition. The sudden-death nature of the tournament tends to induce contestants to play desperately and roughly.

When single elimination is used for outdoor sports, weather delays often cause inconvenient scheduling problems. A complete schedule with all dates and times cannot be printed because postponed games, with few exceptions, must be played the following day if the tournament is to continue in orderly fashion. Round robin schedules are better suited for outdoor sports since a day's schedule can be postponed until the first convenient date for replay. The type of single elimination bracket that works best for outdoor activities is one in which deadline dates are set for each round of play, and contestants contact each other to arrange match times.

Calculations in this section assume that no postponements are possible, and that no entry plays more than once per day.

Given N, the number of entries in the tournament, the following determinations can be made:

Number of games in the tournament $= N - 1$

Example: $N = 15$

number of games $= N - 1$
$$= 15 - 1$$
$$= 14$$

Number of byes in the tournament $=$ (next higher power of two)* $- N$

Example: $N = 23$

next higher power of two $= 32$

number of byes $= 32 - N$
$$= 32 - 23$$
$$= 9$$

Number of first-round games in the tournament $= N -$ (next lower power of two)**

Example: $N = 23$

next lower power of two $= 16$

number of first-round games $= N - 16$
$$= 23 - 16$$
$$= 7$$

The number of rounds in the tournament is outlined by the chart below.

N	next higher power of two	rounds
2	2	1
3	4	2
6	8	3
14	16	4
25	32	5
51	64	6

*Powers of two proceed as follows: 2, 4, 8, 16, 32, 64, etc.

**This is true except when the number of entries is a power of two. The number of first-round games then equals $N \div 2$.

THE BRACKETS — THREE DRAWS

NOTE: No byes occur past the first round. All rounds subsequent to the first round are powers of two.

Draw 1
Example: N = 11

Determine the next higher power of two, 16 in this case, and draw that many lines to establish the first round. Connect those lines and appropriately draw the subsequent rounds. Contestants and byes are placed where desired.

Comment: This bracket consumes much time and space in drawing. It is unnecessary to actually insert the byes and the lines on which they occur. The draws which follow are more economical.

The Type 2 Draw can be quickly sketched. Note that, as indicated in the left margin opposite, the bracket can be broken down to small groups of twos and threes. All brackets, regardless of size, can be broken down to twos, threes, and fours. The appropriate breakdown is achieved by continually halving the number of entries until twos, threes, or fours appear. Odd numbers are divided approximately.

In the example opposite (N = 11), eleven is split into groups of six and five (for consistency, always place the larger number first), six splits to three and three, and five splits to three and two. The diagram below illustrates what has happened.

$$11$$
$$6\text{-}5$$
$$3\text{-}3\text{-}3\text{-}2$$

As shown opposite, the bracket for eleven was drawn with 3 threes and 1 two, in that order. Note that a three cannot be further divided, and that the breakdown is finished at the line where threes appear. The final line can have only two possible combinations of numbers: twos and threes, or fours and threes. Also note that twos are always drawn as second-round games. Fours, as illustrated in the next example, are drawn as two first-round games.

Draw 2

Example: N = 11

Comment: Fewer lines are drawn for a more compact bracket than Draw 1. Contestants C, F, I, J, and K have first-round byes. This type draw could be somewhat confusing to read. The distinction between first- and second-round games might not be clear at first glance.

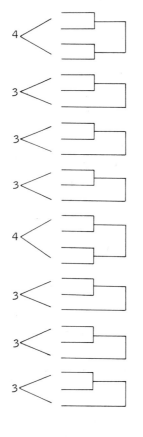

Example: $N = 26$

26

13-13

7-6-7-6

4-3-3-3-4-3-3-3

When all the elements of the last line of the breakdown are drawn, the second round is complete and a function of two. There are no byes remaining and no stranded lines.

The connection of lines for the subsequent rounds is all that remains to be done.

Draw 3

Example: N = 11

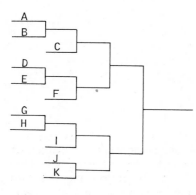

Rd 1   Rd 2   Rd 3   Rd 4

Comment: The bracket is still compact; but now byes and first- and second-round games are readily apparent. This type draw seems most appropriate for the final printed schedule.

NUMBERING THE GAMES

Example: N = 10

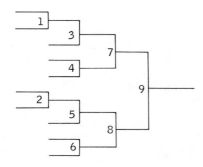

Proceed through each round in numerical order.

Seeding proceeds by alternating placements in halves, and then quarters, of the bracket. The top seed is placed on the top line of the bracket, and the second seed is placed on the bottom line. The third seed goes on the bottom line of the upper half of the bracket, and the fourth seed goes on the top line of the lower half of the bracket. The fifth seed is placed on the bottom line of the upper quarter of the bracket, and the sixth seed is placed on the top line of the lower quarter of the bracket. The seventh seed goes on the top line of the second quarter of the bracket, and the eighth seed goes on the bottom line of the third quarter of the bracket.

SEEDING — TWO METHODS

NOTE: Seeding attempts to provide even competition by separating the top entries and preventing them from meeting in the early rounds. Where byes are available, they are given to the seeded teams in seeded order.

Method 1

Example: *N = 16.*   Eight seeds are desired.

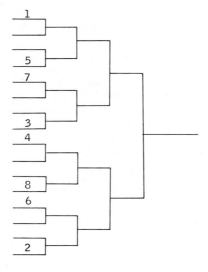

Example: $N = 25$. Eight seeds are desired.

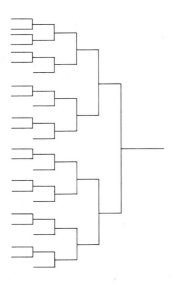

Normally, the bracket is drawn as it appears to the left. When seeding, however, the seeded entries should be given the available byes while still appearing on the appropriate lines of the bracket. The positions of certain lines and groups of lines must be altered to accommodate the seeding procedure. As shown on the opposite page, this is done without altering the "sense" of the bracket.

$N = 25$

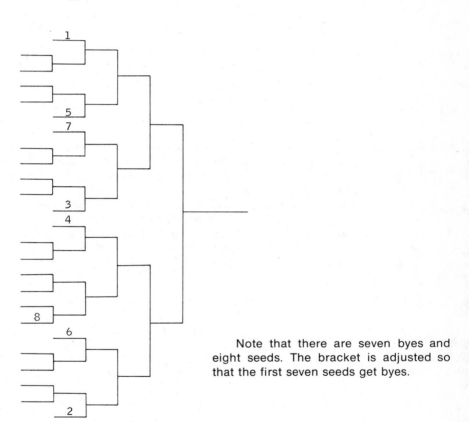

Note that there are seven byes and eight seeds. The bracket is adjusted so that the first seven seeds get byes.

The top seed goes to the top of the bracket, and the second seed is placed at the bottom. The third seed is placed at the top of the lower half of the bracket, and the fourth seed goes to the bottom of the upper half of the bracket.

Note that the seeds at each extreme of the two bracket halves add up to five $(1 + 4, 3 + 2)$. The remaining four seeds are placed opposite the top four seeds so that each pair adds up to nine $(1 + 8, 5 + 4, 3 + 6, 7 + 2)$. The pairings occur in the four quarters of the bracket.

Method 2

Example: $N = 16$.   Eight seeds are desired.

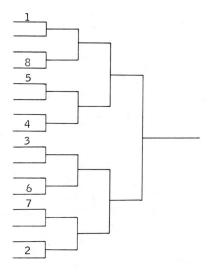

Example: N = 13

Note that there are three byes and eight seeds. The bracket is adjusted so that the top three seeds get byes.

TOURNAMENT PROBLEM-SOLVING

NOTE: There are three factors, or variables, that require consideration in solving tournament problems. They are: (1) N, the number of entries, (2) the number of days needed to run the tournament, and (3) the number of games available for play each day. By predetermining any two of the variables, one can solve for the third. The third variable, games per day, is determined by multiplying the number of courts or fields available times the frequency of their use.

Example: Three courts are available for basketball, and four sessions of games are to be played on each court.

$$\text{Games/day} = \text{number of courts} \times \text{frequency of use}$$
$$= 3 \times 4$$
$$= 12$$

Problem Type I

Example 1

Given: the number of entries (25), and the number of games that can be played each day (4). What minimum number of days is needed to run the tournament?*

Step (1) Determine the number of first-round games.

$$\text{first-round games} = N - \text{lower power of two}$$
$$= 25 - 16$$
$$= 9$$

Step (2) Set up the number of rounds and the number of games for each round. When the number for first-round games

---

*Remember, all solutions to problems are based on the assumption that no entry plays more than once per day.

has been appropriately designated, start with the last round (one game) and work backwards with multiples of two.

round	1	2	3	4	5
games	9	8	4	2	1

Step (3) Determine the number of days needed to play round by round. Start with the last round and work backwards. Eliminate those rounds which obviously take only one day to play (when the games per day are greater than, or equal to, the number of games in a round, place a 1 under that round).

round	1	2	3	4	5
games	9	8	4	2	1
days			1	1	1

NOTE: These are not necessarily the only rounds that can be played in one day. Also, because an entry cannot play more than once per day, no two full rounds can be played in one day.

Step (4) Start with the first round and determine the number of days required to play each round.

There are nine first-round games, and four games can be played per day. Therefore, three days are required to play the first round. Since a total of 12 games could be played in three days, three possible games remain which can be used for games in the second round.

round	1	2	3	4	5
games	9	8	4	2	1
		$\dfrac{-3}{5}$			
days	3		1	1	1

Five games remain in round 2, and these require two days to complete.

round	1	2	3	4	5
games	9	8	4	2	1
		$\dfrac{-3}{5}$			
days	3	2	1	1	1

The total number of days required to run the tournament is determined by adding the last line horizontally.

Answer: Eight days to run the tournament.

Example 2

Given: $N = 17$, and nine games can be played per day. How many days are required to run the tournament?

Step (1)   First-round games $= 17 - 16$
$$= 1$$

Step (2)

round	1	2	3	4	5
games	1	8	4	2	1

Step (3)   Since nine games per day are available, each round can be played in one day.

round	1	2	3	4	5
games	1	8	4	2	1
days	1	1	1	1	1

Answer: Five days needed to run tournament.

Note again that no two full rounds (for instance, the first and second rounds) can be combined for play in one day. This would necessitate the play of one entry twice in one day.

Also note that a single elimination tournament can be run in a minimum number of days when the games available per day equal, or exceed, the number of games in the largest round. The minimum number of days is always equal to the number of rounds in the tournament.

Example 3

Three tournaments are to be run simultaneously.
Given: $N = 36, 25, 14$, and six games can be played per day.
What minimum number of days is required to run the tournaments?

Step (1) Determine the number of first-round games for each tournament.

$$\text{first-round games} = 36 - 32$$
$$= 4$$

$$\text{first-round games} = 25 - 16$$
$$= 9$$

$$\text{first-round games} = 14 - 8$$
$$= 6$$

Step (2) Set up the number of rounds and games for each round of each tournament. Add vertically to arrive at the total number of games in each round.

	round	1	2	3	4	5	6
$N = 36$	games	4	16	8	4	2	1
$N = 25$	games		9	8	4	2	1
$N = 14$	games			6	4	2	1
	total games	4	25	22	12	6	3

Step (3) With six games available for play each day, eliminate as many final rounds as possible.

round	1	2	3	4	5	6
total games	4	25	22	12	6	3
days					1	1

Step (4) Start with the first round and eliminate the remaining rounds.

round	1	2	3	4	5	6
	4	25	22	12	6	3
total games		-2	-1	-5		
		23	21	7		
days	1	4	4	2	1	1

Care must be taken to avoid scheduling entries for play more than once per day.

Answer: Thirteen days are required to run the combined tournament.

/

Problem Type II

Example 1

Given: the number of entries (39), and six days are available to run the tournament.

What is the minimum capability of games available per day required to run the tournament?

Step (1)   Establish the number of rounds and the number of games in each round.

round	1	2	3	4	5	6
games	7	16	8	4	2	1

Step (2)   Divide the number of days available (6) into the number of games in the tournament ($N - 1 = 38$). This operation results in the first index number, which is 7 (always round off to the higher number). Working backward from the last round, recognize those rounds whose number of games is less than the index number 7. These rounds can be played in one day.

round	1	2	3	4	5	6
games	7	16	8	4	2	1
days				1	1	1

Step (3)   Three days have been used to play the last seven games. Divide the remaining number of days (3) into the remaining number of games (31). The result is the second index number, which is 11. Still working backward, recognize those rounds whose number of games is less than 11. One day is required to play each of these rounds. Note that round 2 cannot be circumvented to get to round 1.

round	1	2	3	4	5	6
games	7	16	8	4	2	1
days			1	1	1	1

Step (4)   Four days have been used to play the last 15 games. Divide the remaining number of days (2) into the remaining number of games (23). The third index number is 12.

Twelve is smaller than the number of games (16) in round two. When this occurs, the index number becomes the answer to the problem.

Answer: Twelve games per day are required to run the tournament in six days.

Example 2

Given: $N = 34$, and five days are available to run the tournament.
What capability of games played per day is required to run the tournament?

Step (1) Establish the rounds and the number of games in each round.

rounds   1   2   3   4   5   6

The solution to the problem can be halted with the determination of the number of rounds in the tournament. Six rounds cannot be played in five days without having entries play more than once per day. At least six days are required. Therefore, there is no solution to the problem.

Answer: The tournament is impossible to run under the given conditions.

Example 3

Given: the number of entries (39).
What number of games must be available per day to run the tournament in the minimum number of days?

Step (1) Determine the number of games in the first and second rounds of the tournament.

$$\text{first-round games} = 39 - 32$$
$$= 7$$

$$\text{second-round games} = 32 \div 2$$
$$= 16$$

Step (2) Add the first- and second-round games and divide by two to find the required games per day (this procedure holds when there are fewer first round games than second round games).

$$7 + 16 = 23$$

$$23 \div 2 = 11\frac{1}{2} \quad \text{round off to higher number}$$

Answer: Twelve games must be available per day to run the tournament in the minimum number of days.

When the number of first-round games is greater than or equal to the number of second-round games, the required games per day is equal to the number of games in the first round.

Example: N = 14

$$\text{first-round games} \begin{aligned} &= 14 - 8 \\ &= 6 \end{aligned}$$

$$\text{second-round games} \begin{aligned} &= 8 \div 2 \\ &= 4 \end{aligned}$$

6 games per day are required.

Problem Type III

Given: the number of days available to run the tournament (5), and the number of games that can be played per day (9).

What is the maximum number of entries that can be accommodated within those restrictions?

Step (1) Multiply the number of available days (5) times the number of games that can be played each day (9).

$$9 \times 5 = 45$$

This represents the total number of possible games that could be played under the given conditions.

Step (2) Set up the maximum number of rounds and the maximum number of games for each round. The maximum number of rounds is always equal to the number of days available.

round	1	2	3	4	5
maximum games	16	8	4	2	1

Step (3) Nine games can be played each round. Working backward from round five, determine the number of wasted games in each round by subtracting from nine the maximum number of games for each round.

When the maximum number of games for a round exceeds or equals the number of games that can be played per day, a 0 is recorded in the wasted games column.

round	1	2	3	4	5
maximum games	16	8	4	2	1
wasted games	0	1	5	7	8

Total games wasted $= 21$

Step (4) Subtract the total wasted games (21) from the total possible games that could be played within the set restrictions (45).

$$45 - 21 = 24$$

This represents the maximum number of games that can actually be played in the tournament.

Step (5) The number of entries that can be accommodated is determined by setting up the appropriate formula.

$$\text{number of games} = N - 1$$

$$24 = N - 1$$

$$1 + 24 = N$$

$$25 = N$$

Answer: Twenty-five entries can be accommodated in the tournament.

PROBLEMS FOR SELF-EXAMINATION
(answers in Appendix B)

1. For a single elimination tournament of 19 entries, show the bracket's numerical breakdown and draw the bracket using the Draw 3 method. How many rounds, games, first-round games, and byes are in the tournament?

2. Do the same for a tournament of 54 entries, but draw only the top half of the bracket.

3. Using both seeding methods, seed five entries in a tournament of 20 entries.

4. Find the minimum number of days required to run a single elimination tournament under the following conditions:

   a. $N = 29$ and games/day $= 5$ b. $N = 45$ and games/day $= 3$
   c. $N = 14$ and games/day $= 6$ d. $N = 87$ and games/day $= 9$
   e. $N = 17, 35, 16, 25$ and games/day $= 7$

5. Find the minimum capability of games available per day required to run a single elimination tournament under the following conditions:

   a. $N = 48$ and days $= 10$ b. $N = 32$ and days $= 7$
   c. $N = 20$ and days $= 4$ d. $N = 37$ and days $= 15$

6. Find the maximum number of entries that can be accommodated in a single elimination tournament under the following conditions:

   a. days $= 7$ and games/day $= 7$
   b. days $= 4$ and games/day $= 8$
   c. days $= 16$ and games/day $= 5$
   d. days $= 8$ and games/day $= 3$

9

Double Elimination Tournament

CONSIDERATIONS

A more acceptable champion than in single elimination is determined because one loss does not eliminate an entry from the tournament.

Each entry is assured of playing at least two contests.

As in single-elimination tournaments, scheduling problems due to weather delays make double elimination impractical for outdoor sports.

Calculations appearing in this section assume that no postponements are possible, and that no entry ever plays more than once per day.

Given, N, the number of entries in the tournament, the following determinations can be made:

Minimum number of games in the tournament $= 2N - 2$

Example: $N = 20$ minimum number of games $= 2N - 2$

$$= 2 \times 20 - 2$$
$$= 40 - 2$$
$$= 38$$

Maximum number of games in the tournament $= 2N - 1$

Example: $N = 20$ maximum number of games $= 2N - 1$

$$= 2 \times 20 - 1$$
$$= 40 - 1$$
$$= 39$$

The difference between the minimum and maximum is one game. This is the extra game that must be played in the event that, in what could have been the final contest, the winner of the loser's bracket defeats the final survivor of the original bracket. For scheduling purposes, it must be assumed that the extra game will be needed. The $2N - 1$ formula is used for problem-solving.

THE BRACKETS — TWO DRAWS

NOTE: Rules of single elimination draw apply for the upper bracket.

Draw 1

Example: N = 16

Upper Bracket

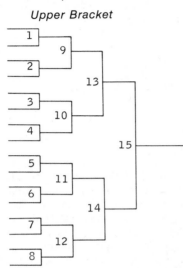

A single elimination bracket (upper bracket) is drawn for 16 entries, and the games are numbered. Since there are 15 games in the bracket, there will be, as the tournament proceeds, 15 losers to be placed in the loser's bracket.

There are eight games in the first round of the upper bracket which, when played, result in eight losers and four first-round games in the lower bracket. Phase 1 of the lower bracket is illustrated below. The playing of the second round of the upper bracket results in four losers. Four lines in the lower bracket must be found on which to add the four losers, and phase 1 of the lower bracket provides them.

Note that, in phase 2, the second round of losers (9–12) is not placed in the lower bracket in numerical order. The halves of the bracket are reversed at that point to delay for as long as possible the meeting of two entries for the second time in the tournament.

The numbers above represent games.

The numbers below represent the losers of the corresponding games in the upper bracket.

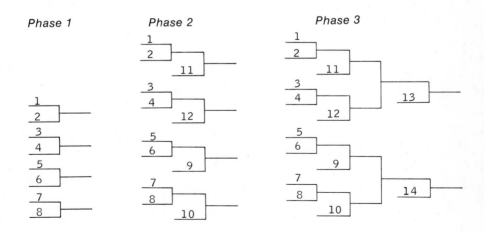

The playing of the third round in the upper bracket results in two losers for which slots must be found in the loser's bracket. Phase 2 of the lower bracket shows four lines; so, two games must be played before the upper-bracket losers can be inserted. The numerical order of their insertion is of no consequence. Phase 3 is illustrated on the preceding page. The final upper-bracket loser remains to be placed, and phase 4 (opposite) shows the placement.

The upper and lower brackets are connected so that the winners of both brackets play each other. A possible extra game is indicated by dotted lines, and the whole double elimination bracket is illustrated on the following page.

Phase 4

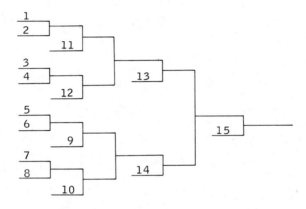

The numbers here represent the losers of the corresponding games in the upper bracket.

OVER-UNDER METHOD OF DRAW

This type draw is referred to in subsequent discussions of double elimination tournaments.

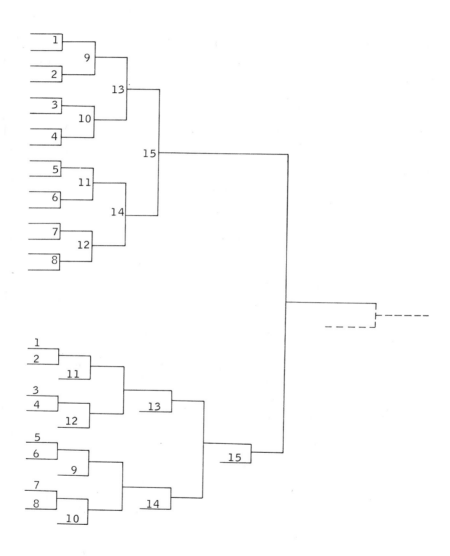

BACK-TO-BACK METHOD OF DRAW

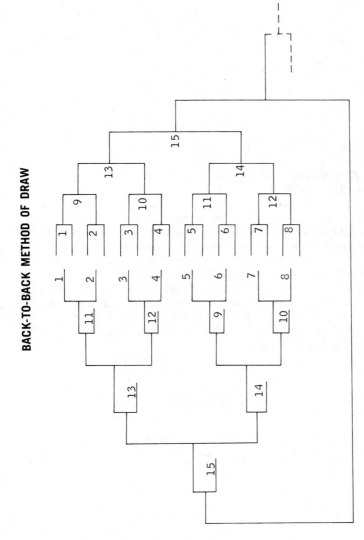

NOTE: This draw is more cumbersome than the over-under style because the loser's bracket must be drawn backwards.

RULES FOR DRAWING BRACKETS
THAT INVOLVE BYES

If there are more first-round games than second-round games in the upper bracket, start the first round of the lower bracket with the first-round losers. When establishing the first round, make sure that the correct number of lines is available to accommodate pairings with the second-round losers of the upper bracket.

If the second round of the upper bracket is greater than or equal to the first round, combine the first- and second-round losers and start the lower bracket with them. This time, keep in mind the number of third-round losers from the upper bracket that must be inserted in the lower bracket.

Example: N = 10

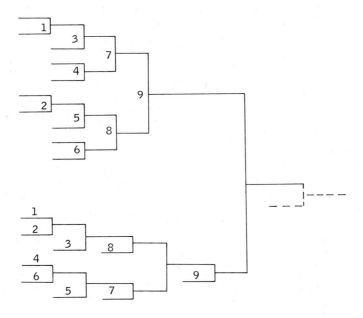

Example: N = 13

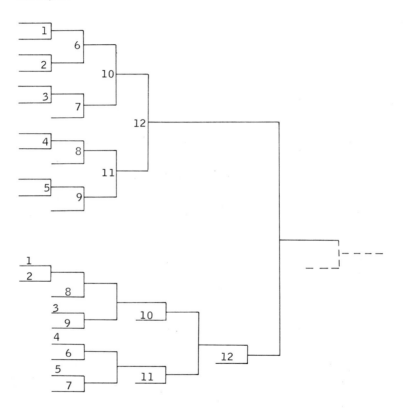

TOURNAMENT PROBLEM-SOLVING

Preliminary Considerations

A double elimination tournament for 32 entries is illustrated on the following pages. The game numbers in the upper bracket are those without parentheses. The numbers without parentheses in the lower bracket represent the losers of the corresponding games in the upper bracket. The numbers in parentheses indicate days of play, and rounds of play, in reverse order. For example, an (8) means that the game for which it appears is played on the eighth to last day, and in the eighth to last round, of the tournament. A (1) indicates the last day, and round, of the tournament. Note that in order to denote days of play equal to rounds of play, the games available per day must be equal to the number of games in the largest round of the tournament.

The solutions to problems involving double elimination tournaments are best understood by working backward from the last game to the first round of the upper bracket. By working backward, the final rounds of a double elimination tournament can be standardized, just as those for single elimination tournaments are standardized. Single elimination brackets are drawn so that every round beyond the first round is a perfect round (i.e., a power of two), except the last round, which is only one game. Double elimination is more complicated, but the same concept can be applied.

A look at both the bracket (on following pages) and the chart (below) shows that regardless of the number of games to be played per day, the last three games require one day each to play. Should two or more games per day be available, the last seven games can be played in five days. With four or more games available per day, the last 15 games can be played in seven days. Eight or more games allow the last 31 games to be played in nine days. Sixteen or more games allow the last 63 games to be played in 11 days.

Games Available per Day	Number of Days to Play Last Number of Games	Maximum Games for Each Round of Play (rounds in reverse order)										
		11	10	9	8	7	6	5	4	3	2	1
2–3	5 days for last 7 games							2	2	1	1	1
4–7	7 days for last 15 games					4	4	2	2	1	1	1
8–15	9 days for last 31 games			8	8	4	4	2	2	1	1	1
16–31	11 days for last 63 games	16	16	8	8	4	4	2	2	1	1	1

Perfect rounds of play are established for double elimination tournaments of 4, 8, 16, and 32 entries. For example, the chart shows that a tournament for eight entries requires 15 games and has seven rounds of play. A tournament for 16 entries requires 31 games and has nine rounds of play.

From the chart, then, ratios can be set up and employed in establishing rounds of play and in solving tournament problems involving any number of entries.

Games Per Day	Ratio
2–3	5/7
4–7	7/15
8–15	9/31
16–31	11/63

When establishing rounds of play, it must be noted that certain games in the upper bracket must be played before other games in the lower bracket. For instance, upper bracket games 25, 26, 27, and 28 must be played before those games in the lower bracket which involve the losers of the upper-bracket games. When working backward, therefore, the round in the loser's bracket, indicated by (7), is considered before the corresponding round in the upper bracket (8).

Rounds of play for tournaments which involve nonperfect rounds are established in the following manner.

Example: N = 14

Step (1) Determine the number of games in the tournament.

$$\text{number of games} = 2N - 1$$
$$= 2 \times 14 - 1$$
$$= 28 - 1$$
$$= 27$$

Step (2) Select the appropriate ratio — one whose number of games comes closest to the number of games in the tournament without exceeding that number.

Ratio: 7/15

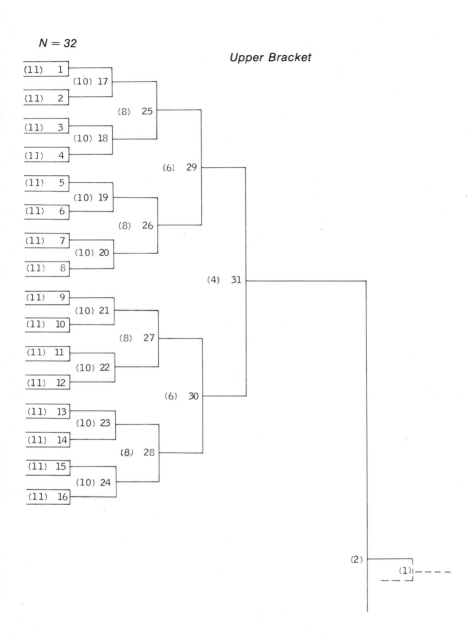

N = *32*

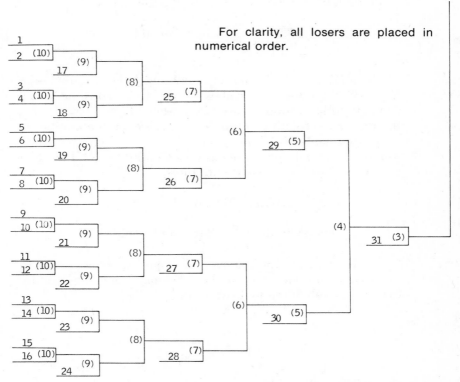

Lower Bracket

For clarity, all losers are placed in numerical order.

Reminder: The numbers in parentheses, while denoting days of play in reverse order, also indicate rounds of play in reverse order. For purposes of explanation, it is assumed that sufficient games can be played per day so that each round is playable in one day.

Step (3) The ratio immediately establishes the final seven rounds of the tournament.

round	1	2	3	4	5	6	7
games	4	4	2	2	1	1	1

Step (4) Subtract those games (15) already accounted for from the total number of games in the tournament.

$$27 - 15 = 12 \text{ games remaining}$$

Step (5) If the number of remaining games is equal to or less than the number of games in the last established round (seventh to last round in this case), establish the first round of the tournament with that number. If, however, the number of remaining games is greater than those in the last established round, the remaining games are divided by two and the first two rounds are established with those numbers.

$$\text{remaining games} = 12$$

$$\text{games in the last established round} = 4$$

Under the rule set forth above, the appropriate procedure in this case is to divide the number of remaining games (12) by two and establish the first two rounds.

$$12/2 = 6$$

The total sequence of rounds is:

round	1	2	3	4	5	6	7	8	9
games	6	6	4	4	2	2	1	1	1

$$\text{number of rounds} = 9$$

$$\text{total games} = 27$$

Example: $N = 19$

Step (1)

$$\text{number of games} = 2N - 1$$
$$= 2 \times 19 - 1$$
$$= 38 - 1$$
$$= 37$$

Step (2) Appropriate ratio is 9/31.

Step (3) The final nine rounds are established.

round	1	2	3	4	5	6	7	8	9
games	8	8	4	4	2	2	1	1	1

Step (4) $37 - 31 = 6$ games remaining

Step (5) Six games is less than those (8) in the last established round. Therefore, the first round consists of six games, and the total sequence of rounds is as follows:

round	1	2	3	4	5	6	7	8	9	10
games	6	8	8	4	4	2	2	1	1	1

$$\text{number of rounds} = 10$$
$$\text{total games} = 37$$

Problem Type I

Example 1

Given: the number of entries (13) and the number of games that can be played per day (4).

What minimum number of days is needed to run the tournament?

Step (1) Determine the number of games in the tournament.

$$\text{number of games} = 2N - 1$$
$$= 2 \times 13 - 1$$
$$= 26 - 1$$
$$= 25$$

Step (2) Determine the largest round of the touranment.

The largest round of a double elimination tournament is determined as either the first or second round of the upper bracket.

Since the upper bracket is a simple single elimination draw, the numbers of first- and second-round games are found as follows:

$$\text{first-round games} = N - \text{next lower power of two}$$
$$= 13 - 8$$
$$= 5$$

$$\text{second-round games} = \text{next lower power of two} \div 2$$
$$= 8 \div 2$$
$$= 4$$

The largest round of the tournament, therefore, is the first round, which has five games. Since the number of games played per day cannot exceed the largest round of the tournament, the games per day must be less than or equal to the number of games in the largest round. Should a situation arise in which the number of games available per day exceeds the largest round, simply reduce the games per day to equal the number of games in the largest round.

$$\text{games/day} = 4$$
$$\text{largest round} = 5$$
$$\text{no adjustment necessary}$$

Step (3) Establish a ratio that corresponds to the games played per day, and subtract the number of games in that ratio from the number of games in the tournament to find the games remaining.

With 4 games per day, the appropriate ratio is 7/15.

$$\begin{array}{r} 25 \\ \underline{7/15} \\ 10 \text{ games remaining} \end{array}$$

Step (4) Find the days needed to play the remaining number of games by dividing the remaining games by the games played per day. Always round off to higher number.

$$10 \div 4 = 3 \text{ days}$$

Step (5) Add the number of days used in the ratio and the days found in step (4) to arrive at the number of days needed to run the tournament.

$$\text{number of days} = 7 + 3$$
$$= 10$$

Answer: Ten days are required to run the tournament.

For the purposes of calculation and illustration of calculation, double elimination tournaments are developed in reverse order. This procedure usually results in something similar to what has occurred in the illustration opposite. The first round of the tournament has only two designated games, even though four games are available per day. In the actual scheduling of double elimination play, it is quite likely that the sequence of games played will be different from what appears opposite. The logical procedure is to play four first-round games rather than two, as indicated.

Example 1   Sequence of Play in Reverse Order

days	10	9	8	7	6	5	4	3	2	1
games	2	4	4	4	4	2	2	1	1	1

Numbers in parentheses represent days of play in reverse order.

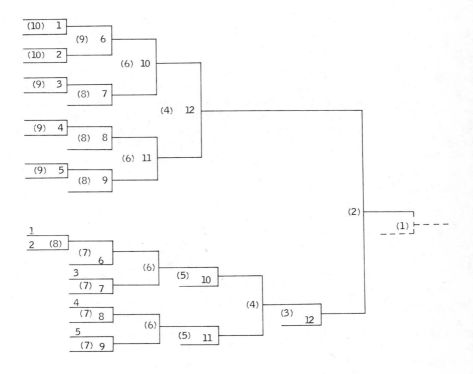

The actual schedule of play could be developed in the manner depicted opposite. Although the sequences of play between the actual schedule and the reverse-order calculation might be different, the answer to the original question (how many days are required to run the tournament?) remains the same—10 days.

Example 1A   Sequence of Play in Normal Order.

days	1	2	3	4	5	6	7	8	9	10
games	4	4	4	4	3	2	1	1	1	1

Numbers in parentheses represent days of play in normal sequence.

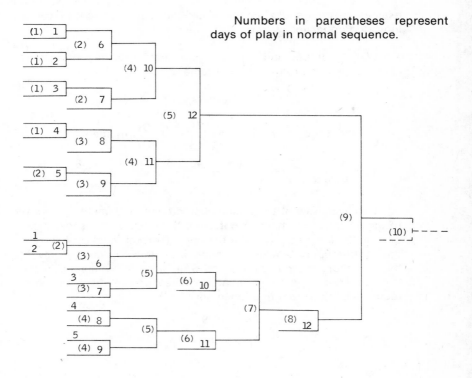

Caution: Even though solutions to double elimination problems are valid, care must be taken to insure that the numbers for games and game losers are correctly placed in the bracket. An example of what could happen if numbers are incorrectly placed is indicated opposite.

With 10 entries and four games available per day, how many days are required to run the tournament?

total games = 19

Eight days are required to run the tournament.

days	1	2	3	4	5	6	7	8
games	4	4	4	2	2	1	1	1

Careless draw of the bracket could result in something similar to the incorrect tournament opposite. Note that on the second day of play, the loser of game 5 in the upper bracket must play twice— once in the upper bracket and once in the lower bracket. To avoid that situation, the numbers 5 and 6 must be interchanged in the lower bracket. The tournament may then proceed with no entry required to play more than once per day.

Numbers in parentheses indicate days
of play in normal sequence.

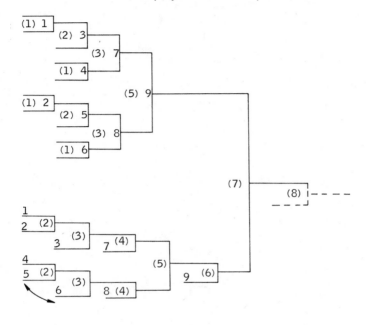

Correct draw would have these two
numbers interchanged.

Example 2

Given: $N = 13$, and nine games are available for play each day.

What minimum number of days is required to run the tournament?

Step (1)

$$\text{number of games} = 2N - 1$$
$$= 2 \times 13 - 1$$
$$= 26 - 1$$
$$= 25$$

Step (2)

$$\text{first-round games} = 13 - 8$$
$$= 5$$

$$\text{second-round games} = 8 \div 2$$
$$= 4$$

$$\text{largest round} = 5$$
$$\text{games/day} = 9$$

The number of games that can be played per day must be reduced from nine to five.

Step (3)

$$\begin{array}{r} 25 \\ 7/\overline{15} \\ \overline{10} \text{ games remain} \end{array}$$

Step (4)

$$10 \div 5 = 2 \text{ days}$$

Step (5)

$$7 + 2 = 9$$

Answer: Nine days are required to run the tournament.

Example 3

Given: $N = 23$

What minimum number of games per day must be available in order to run the tournament in a minimum number of days? How many days are needed to run the tournament?

Step (1)

$$\text{number of games} = 2N - 1$$
$$= 2 \times 23 - 1$$
$$= 46 - 1$$
$$= 45$$

Step (2)

$$\text{first-round games} = 23 - 16$$
$$= 7$$
$$\text{second-round games} = 16 \div 2$$
$$= 8$$

The largest round is eight, so eight games must be available per day.

Step (3)

$$\begin{array}{r} 45 \\ 9/\overline{31} \\ \hline 14 \text{ games remain} \end{array}$$

Step (4)

$$14 \div 8 = 2 \text{ days}$$

Step (5)

$$9 + 2 = 11$$

Answer: Eleven days are needed to run the tournament.

NOTE: The solution to the above problem can also be used to determine the number of rounds in the tournament.

Example 4

Three tournaments are to be run simultaneously.
Given: $N = 10, 19, 36$, and seven games can be played
    per day.
How many days are required to run the tournaments?

Step (1)   Determine the number of games for each tournament.

$$\text{number of games} = 2N - 1$$
$$= 2 \times 10 - 1$$
$$= 20 - 1$$
$$= 19$$

$$\text{number of games} = 2N - 1$$
$$= 2 \times 19 - 1$$
$$= 38 - 1$$
$$= 37$$

$$\text{number of games} = 2N - 1$$
$$= 2 \times 36 - 1$$
$$= 72 - 1$$
$$= 71$$

Step (2)   Set up the number of rounds and games for each round of each tournament. Add vertically to get the total number of games for each round.

round	1	2	3	4	5	6	7	8	9	10	11	12
games ($N = 10$)					4	4	4	2	2	1	1	1
games ($N = 19$)			6	8	8	4	4	2	2	1	1	1
games ($N = 36$)	8	16	16	8	8	4	4	2	2	1	1	1
total games	8	16	22	16	20	12	12	6	6	3	3	3

Step (3) With seven games available for play each day, eliminate as many final rounds as possible.

round	1	2	3	4	5	6	7	8	9	10	11	12
total games	8	16	22	16	20	12	12	6	6	3	3	3
days								1	1	1	1	1

Step (4) Start with the first round and eliminate the remaining rounds.

NOTE: Because of the complicated nature of double elimination play, special care must be taken to avoid scheduling entries for play more than once per day. Particular problems occur in this regard when large numbers of games can be played per day. Large numbers often allow the scheduling of an invalid number of games per day. In the interests of caution and speed of calculation, therefore, it is suggested that games be scheduled conservatively. When complications and doubt arise during the process of calculating numbers of days to complete rounds of play, days should be assigned liberally to "play it safe." This procedure may or may not result in the absolute minimum number of days required to run the tournaments, but a quick, relatively accurate estimation is achieved. Further, the established estimate is always one where, in actual scheduling, no additional days are ever required to run the tournaments. To the contrary, one or two less than estimated may be sufficient.

round	1	2	3	4	5	6	7	8	9	10	11	12
total games	8	16 −6 / 10	22 −4 / 18	16 −3 / 13	20 −1 / 19	12 −2 / 10	12 −4 / 8	6	6	3	3	3
days	2	2	3	2	3	2	2	1	1	1	1	1

Answer: Twenty-one days are required to run the tournaments.

Problem Type II

Example 1

Given: the number of entries (12), and the number of days available to run the tournament (10).

What is the minimum capability of games played per day necessary to run the tournament?

Step (1) Determine the number of games in the tournament.

$$\text{number of games} = 2N - 1$$
$$= 2 \times 12 - 1$$
$$= 24 - 1$$
$$= 23$$

Step (2) Divide the number of games by the number of days available. This results in an index number which, in turn, indicates the appropriate ratio. Index numbers are considered as games per day when related to ratios; so an index of three would result in a 5/7 ratio, and an index of 6 a 7/15 ratio. Always round off to higher number.

$$23 \div 10 = 3$$

5/7 ratio is appropriate

Step (3) Subtract the number of final games in the ratio from the games in the tournament.

$$\begin{array}{r} 23 \\ \underline{5/7} \\ 16 \text{ games remain} \end{array}$$

Step (4) Five days have been used to play the last seven games. Divide the remaining number of days (5) into the remaining number of games (16) to find the required number of games that must be available per day. Always round off to higher number.

$$16 \div 5 = 4$$

Four is the correct answer as long as it does not exceed the number of games in the largest round. The largest round of the tournament is four.

Answer: Four games per day must be available to run the tournament.

Example 2

Given: $N = 8$, and 6 days are available to run the tournament.

Find the minimum number of games per day required to run the tournament.

Step (1)

$$\text{number of games} = 2N - 1$$
$$= 2 \times 8 - 1$$
$$= 16 - 1$$
$$= 15$$

Step (2)

$$15 \div 6 = 3 \text{ (index number)}$$

Step (3)

$$\begin{array}{r} 15 \\ 5/7 \\ \hline 8 \text{ games remaining} \\ 1 \text{ day remaining} \end{array}$$

Step (4)

$$8 \div 1 = 8 \text{ games/day}$$

The answer is incorrect because eight is greater than the largest round of the tournament (4). The tournament is impossible to run in six days. This conclusion could have been reached immediately by noting that it takes at least seven days to play the last 15 games.

If seven days were available, then:

Step (2a)

$$15 \div 7 = 3 \text{ (index number)}$$

Step (3a)

$$
\begin{array}{r}
15 \\
\underline{5/7} \\
\end{array}
$$
8 games remaining
2 days remaining

Step (4a)

$$8 \div 2 = 4$$

Answer: Four games per day must be available to run the tournament.

Problem Type III

Example 1

Given: the number of days available to run the tournament (10), and the number of games that can be played per day (4).

What is the maximum number of entries that can be accommodated in the tournament?

Step (1) The number of games per day (4) leads to a ratio of 7/15.

Step (2) Seven days have been used to play 15 games. Determine the remaining days, and multiply them times the available games per day (4) to find the number of possible remaining games.

$$10 - 7 = 3 \text{ days remaining}$$

$$3 \times 4 = 12 \text{ games remaining}$$

Step (3) Add the number of remaining games (12) to the number of games in the ratio (15) to find the number of games in the tournament.

$$12 + 15 = 27 \text{ games}$$

Step (4)   Inject the number of games (27) into the formula to find N.

$$2N - 1 = 27$$
$$2N = 27 + 1$$
$$N = 28 \div 2$$
$$N = 14$$

Before accepting the answer as correct, determine the largest round in the tournament and check it against the games per day. If the games per day is greater than the largest round, the answer is incorrect.

$$\text{games per day} = \mathbf{4}$$
$$\text{largest round} = \mathbf{6}$$

Answer: Fourteen entries can play in the tournament.

Example 2

Given: Ten days are available to run the tournament, and three games may be played per day.
Find the maximum number of entries that can play in the tournament.

Step (1)   Three games per day leads to a ratio of 5/7.

Step (2)

$$10 - 5 = 5 \text{ days remaining}$$
$$5 \times 3 = 15 \text{ games remaining}$$

Step (3)

$$7 + 15 = 22 \text{ games in the tournament}$$

Step (4)

$$2N - 1 = 22$$
$$2N = 22 + 1$$
$$N = 23 \div 2$$
$$N = 11\frac{1}{2} \quad \text{(round off to lower number)}$$
$$N = 11$$

$$\text{games per day} = 3$$

$$\text{largest round} = 4$$

Answer: Eleven entries can be accommodated in the tournament.

Example 3

Given: Eight days are available to run the tournament, and the availability of seven games per day exists.

How many entries can play in the tournament?

Step (1) Seven games per day leads to a ratio of 7/15.

Step (2)

$$8 - 7 = 1 \text{ day remaining}$$
$$1 \times 7 = 7 \text{ games remaining}$$

Step (3)

$$7 + 15 = 22 \text{ games in the tournament}$$

Step (4)

$$2N - 1 = 22$$
$$2N = 22 + 1$$
$$N = 23 \div 2$$
$$N = 11\frac{1}{2}$$
$$N = 11$$

$$\text{games per day} = 7$$

$$\text{largest round} = 4$$

Answer is invalid and the tournament cannot be run under the given circumstances. The number of games per day must be reduced until the correct answer is found.

Try five games per day.

Step (1a)   Five games per day leads to a ratio of 7/15.

Step (2a)

$$8 - 7 = 1 \text{ day remaining}$$

$$1 \times 5 = 5 \text{ remaining games}$$

Step (3a)

$$15 + 5 = 20 \text{ games in the tournament}$$

Step (4a)

$$2N - 1 = 20$$

$$2N = 20 + 1$$

$$N = 21 \div 2$$

$$N = 10\frac{1}{2}$$

$$N = 10$$

$$\text{games per day} = 5$$

$$\text{largest round} = 4$$

Answer is still incorrect.
Try four games per day.

Step (1b)   Four games per day leads to a ratio of 7/15.

Step (2b)

$$8 - 7 = 1 \text{ day remaining}$$

$$1 \times 4 = 4 \text{ games remaining}$$

Step (3b)

$$4 + 15 = 19 \text{ games in the tournament}$$

Step (4b)

$$2N - 1 = 19$$

$$2N = 19 + 1$$

$$N = 20 \div 2$$

$$N = 10$$

games per day $= 4$

largest round $= 4$

Answer: Ten entries may play in the tournament.

PROBLEMS FOR SELF-EXAMINATION
(answers in Appendix B)

1. Draw double elimination tournaments and inject the appropriate numbers for the following situations:

   a. N $= 22$
   b. N $= 6$

2. Set up the sequences of rounds and games per round for double elimination tournaments under the following circumstances:

   a. N $= 11$
   b. N $= 23$
   c. N $= 7$

3. Find the minimum number of days needed to run a double elimination tournament under the following conditions:

   a. N $= 35$ and games/day $= 5$
   b. N $= 25$ and games/day $= 10$
   c. N $= 78$ and games/day $= 12$
   d. N $= 14, 17, 48$ and games/day $= 9$

4. Find the minimum capability of games played per day necessary to run a double elimination tournament under the following conditions:

   a. N $= 20$ and days $= 10$ b. N $= 34$ and days $= 9$
   c. N $= 18$ and days $= 11$ d. N $= 9$ and days $= 9$

5. Find the maximum number of entries that can be accommodated in a double elimination tournament under the following conditions:

   a. days = 14 and games/day = 4
   b. days = 19 and games/day = 10
   c. days = 7 and games/day = 6
   d. days = 11 and games/day = 3

10

Type I Consolation Tournament

CONSIDERATIONS

Type I consolation tournaments consist of one single elimination bracket and one consolation bracket. Only first-game losers are placed in the loser's bracket. This becomes a separate single elimination tournament with its own champion.

The essential intent of type I consolation is to play a regular single elimination tournament and provide extra play for first-game losers. Each entry is assured of playing at least two games.

The only significance of the consolation bracket is that it provides additional competition. No entry in the consolation bracket has a chance at the regular championship.

The tournament is susceptible to forfeits in the consolation bracket since contestants have no chance at the championship.

Because of the infrequent use of this type of tournament, and because of the cumbersome nature of some of the calculations, the extent of the explanation and analysis is limited in this discussion.

Calculations in this section assume that no postponements are possible and that no entry ever plays more than once per day.

145

DRAWING THE BRACKETS

NOTE: The rules of single elimination draw apply for the construction of both the championship and consolation brackets.

Given: $N = 8$

First draw a single elimination for eight entries. Then, determine the number of all possible first-game losers and draw a single elimination consolation bracket.

Because byes are involved in the championship bracket, it is impossible to determine accurately the exact number of first-game losers. At least four first-game losers can be immediately identified as coming from games 1, 2, 4, and 6. However, two more first-game losers might arise from games 3 and 5. Should the entries that had byes lose, the total number of first-game losers would be six. The consolation bracket must, therefore, provide for the maximum possibility of six.

Where possible, byes in the consolation bracket are assigned to entries that had first-round byes in the upper bracket and whose games in the upper bracket could not possibly be played until the second day of competition (i.e., entries that must wait for a first-round winner before playing their first games).

Given N, the number of entries, the number of games in the tournament can be determined. As in double elimination, the maximum number of games is required for scheduling purposes.

Example: N = 10

Championship
 Bracket

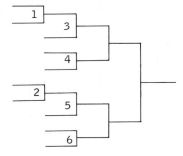

Consolation
 Bracket

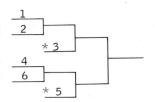

*When no consolation entry is
available, a bye is placed
in this slot.

MAXIMUM NUMBER OF GAMES

Example 1

Given: $N = 13$

Step (1) Determine the number of games in the championship bracket.

$$\text{number of games} = N - 1$$
$$= 13 - 1$$
$$= 12$$

Step (2) Determine the number of first- and second-round games.

$$\text{first-round games} = 13 - 8$$
$$= 5$$

$$\text{second-round games} = 8 \div 2$$
$$= 4$$

Step (3) Since the number of first-round games exceeds the number of second-round games, the maximum number of first-game losers is determined by adding the number of first-round games to the number of byes in the championship bracket.

$$\text{number of byes} = 16 - 13$$
$$= 3$$

maximum number of first-game losers = first round games + byes

$$= 5 + 3$$
$$= 8$$

Step (4) Find the maximum number of games in the consolation bracket.

$$\text{number of games} = N - 1$$
$$= 8 - 1$$
$$= 7$$

Step (5) Add the number of games in both the championship and consolation brackets to arrive at the maximum number of tournament games.

$$\text{tournament games} = \text{championship games} + \text{consolation games}$$
$$= 12 + 7$$
$$= 19$$

Answer: Nineteen maximum games in the tournament.

Example 2

Given: $N = 11$

Step (1)

$$\text{number of games} = N - 1$$
$$= 11 - 1$$
$$= 10$$

Step (2)

$$\text{first-round games} = 11 - 8$$
$$= 3$$

$$\text{second-round games} = 8 \div 2$$
$$= 4$$

Step (3) Since the number of first-round games is less than the number of second-round games, the maximum number of first-game losers is found by adding the numbers of first- and second-round games.

$$\text{maximum number of first-game losers} = \text{first-round games} + \text{second-round games}$$

$$= 3 + 4$$

$$= 7$$

Step (4)

$$\text{maximum consolation games} = N - 1$$

$$= 7 - 1$$

$$= 6$$

Step (5)

$$\text{tournament games} = 10 + 6$$

$$= 16$$

Answer: Sixteen maximum games in the tournament.

Example 3

Given: $N = 12$

Step (1)

$$\text{number of games} = N - 1$$

$$= 12 - 1$$

$$= 11$$

Step (2)

$$\text{first-round games} = 12 - 8$$

$$= 4$$

$$\text{second-round games} = 8 \div 2$$

$$= 4$$

Step (3)   Since the numbers of first- and second-round games are equal, add them to get the maximum number of first-game losers.

maximum first-game losers = first-round games
$$+ \text{ second-round games}$$
$$= 4 + 4$$
$$= 8$$

Step (4)

$$\text{maximum consolation games} = N - 1$$
$$= 8 - 1$$
$$= 7$$

Step (5)

$$\text{tournament games} = 11 + 7$$
$$= 18$$

Answer: Eighteen maximum games in the tournament.

TOURNAMENT PROBLEM-SOLVING

Preliminary Considerations

As in double elimination, the solutions to type I consolation problems are best understood by working backward from the final to the first round.

The chart below describes the relationships between available games per day, ratios, and rounds of play.

GAMES AVAILABLE PER DAY	NUMBER OF DAYS TO PLAY LAST NUMBER OF GAMES	MAXIMUM GAMES FOR EACH ROUND OF PLAY (ROUNDS IN REVERSE ORDER)			
		4	3	2	1
2–3	1 day for last 2 games (1/2)				2
4–7	2 days for last 6 games (2/6)			4	2
8–15	3 days for last 14 games (3/14)		8	4	2
16–31	4 days for last 30 games (4/30)	16	8	4	2

Rounds of play are established in the following manner:

Example: N = 13

Step (1) Determine the number of games and the largest round in the tournament.

$$\text{number of games} = 19$$

$$\text{largest round} = 5$$

Step (2) Use the number of games in the largest round as the games available per day. Determine the appropriate ratio and set up rounds of play to that point.

With five games per day, the appropriate ratio is 2/6.

round	2	1
games	4	2

Step (3) Determine the number of remaining rounds required to complete the tournament. Subtract the number of games in the ratio from the tournament games to find the remaining games. Divide the remaining games by the available games per day.

$$19 - 6 = 13 \text{ games remaining}$$

$$13 \div 5 = 3 \text{ rounds remaining}$$

Step (4) When three rounds remain, the first round of the tournament is the first round of the championship bracket. The second round is the second round of the championship bracket; and the third round consists of the games that remain.

round	1	2	3	4	5
games	5	4	4	4	2

NOTE: When only two rounds remain, divide the remaining games by two and insert the games appropriately in the first two rounds.

Problem Type I

Example 1

Given: the number of entries (15), and the number of games that can be played per day (5).

What minimum number of days is required to run the tournament?

Step (1) Determine the number of games in the tournament.

$$\text{number of championship games} = N - 1$$
$$= 15 - 1$$
$$= 14$$

$$\text{number of first-game losers} = \text{first-round games} + \text{byes}$$
$$= 7 + 1$$
$$= 8$$

$$\text{number of consolation games} = N - 1$$
$$= 8 - 1$$
$$= 7$$

$$\text{tournament games} = 14 + 7$$
$$= 21$$

Step (2) Determine the largest round of the tournament and compare it to the number of available games per day. Where appropriate, games per day must be reduced to equal the largest round of the tournament.

NOTE: The largest round of the tournament is determined as either the first or second round of the championship bracket.

$$\text{games/day} = 5 \qquad \text{largest round} = 7$$

no adjustment necessary

Step (3) Select the appropriate ratio and subtract the number of games in the ratio from the number of games in the tournament to find the remaining games.

With five games per day use the 2/6 ratio (2 days for last 6 games).

$$\begin{array}{r} 21 \\ \underline{2/6} \\ 15 \end{array} \text{ games remaining}$$

Step (4) Divide the remaining number of games by the games played per day to find the number of days required to play the remaining games.

$$15 \div 5 = 3 \text{ days}$$

Step (5) Add the number of days used in the ratio and the days found in step (4) to arrive at the number of days needed to run the tournament.

$$2 + 3 = 5$$

Answer: Five days are required to run the tournament.

Example 1   *N* = 15

Championship
Bracket

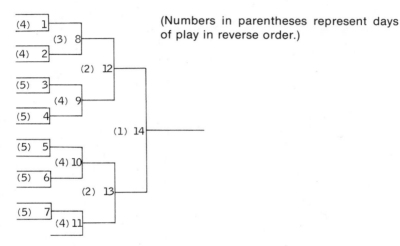

(Numbers in parentheses represent days
of play in reverse order.)

Consolation
Bracket

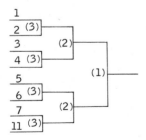

Note the unusual scheduling pattern
in the first two rounds of the championship bracket. For the tournament to be run
in five days, game 7 must be played on the
first day, game 11 on the second day, and
the loser of game 11 plays in the consolation bracket on the third day.

Example 2

Given: $N = 16$, and nine games can be played per day. How many days are required to run the tournament?

Step (1)

$$\text{number of championship games} = N - 1$$
$$= 16 - 1$$
$$= 15$$

$$\text{number of first-game losers} = 8 \text{ (perfect round)}$$

$$\text{number of consolation games} = N - 1$$
$$= 8 - 1$$
$$= 7$$

$$\text{tournament games} = 15 + 7$$
$$= 22$$

Step (2)

$$\text{games/day} = 9 \qquad \text{largest round} = 8$$
$$\text{must reduce to 8 games/day}$$

Step (3)   Appropriate ratio is 3/14.

$$\frac{22}{3/14}$$
$$\overline{8} \text{ games remaining}$$

Step (4)

$$8 \div 8 = 1 \text{ day}$$

Step (5)

$$3 + 1 = 4$$

Answer: Four days are needed to run the tournament.

Example 3

Three tournaments are to be run simultaneously.

Given: $N = 11, 16, 21$; and 10 games can be played per day.

How many days are required to run the tournaments?

Step (1) Determine the number of games for each tournament.

$$\text{number of games} = 16$$

$$\text{number of games} = 22$$

$$\text{number of games} = 32$$

Step (2) Set up the number of rounds and games for each round of each tournament. Add vertically to get the total number of games for each round.

round	1	2	3	4	5	6
games ($N = 11$)		3	4	3	4	2
games ($N = 16$)			8	8	4	2
games ($N = 21$)	5	8	5	8	4	2
total games	5	11	17	19	12	6

Step (3) With 10 games available for play each day, establish the number of days required to play each round.

round	1	2	3	4	5	6
total games	5	11 $\frac{-5}{6}$	17	19	12	6
days	1	1	2	2	2	1

As with double elimination, the complex nature of type I consolation makes it necessary to be conservative in scheduling games. Where expedient, assign days liberally.

Answer: Nine days are required to run the tournaments.

Problem Type II

Example 1

Given: the number of entries (16), and the number of days available for play (8).

How many games must be available for play each day in order to run the tournament?

Step (1) Determine the number of games in the tournament.

number of championship games $= N - 1$

$$= 16 - 1$$
$$= 15$$

first-game losers $= 8$ (perfect round)

consolation games $= N - 1$

$$= 8 - 1$$
$$= 7$$

tournament games $= 15 + 7$

$$= 22$$

Step (2) Divide the tournament games by the days available for play to find an index number which, in turn, indicates the appropriate ratio. Round off to higher number.

$$22 \div 8 = 3 \text{ (index number)}$$

appropriate ratio 1/2

Step (3) Subtract the number of games in the ratio from the number of tournament games to find the games remaining.

$$\frac{\begin{array}{r} 22 \\ 1/2 \end{array}}{20 \text{ games remaining}}$$

Step (4) Divide the remaining number of days into the remaining number of games to arrive at the required games per day.

$$20 \div 7 = 3 \text{ games/day}$$

The answer must be checked against the largest round of the tournament.

$$\text{games/day} = 3 \qquad \text{largest round} = 8$$

Answer: Three games per day must be available to run the tournament.

Example 2

Given: $N = 11$, and four days are available to run the tournament.

At least how many games must be available per day to run the tournament?

Step (1)

$$\begin{aligned} \text{championship games} &= N - 1 \\ &= 11 - 1 \\ &= 10 \end{aligned}$$

$$\begin{aligned} \text{first-game losers} &= \text{first-round games} + \text{second-round games} \\ &= 3 + 4 \\ &= 7 \end{aligned}$$

$$\begin{aligned} \text{consolation games} &= N - 1 \\ &= 7 - 1 \\ &= 6 \end{aligned}$$

$$\begin{aligned} \text{tournament games} &= 10 + 6 \\ &= 16 \end{aligned}$$

Step (2)

$$16 \div 4 = 4 \text{ (index number)}$$

appropriate ratio is 2/6

Step (3)

$$\begin{array}{l} 16 \\ \underline{2/6} \\ 10 \text{ games remain} \end{array}$$

Step (4)

$$10 \div 2 = 5 \text{ games/day}$$

largest round $= 4$

Tournament is impossible to run in the given number of days. The number of days must be increased.
Try five days in which to run the tournament.

Step (2a)

$$16 \div 5 = 4 \text{ (index number)}$$

appropriate ratio is 2/6

Step (3a)

$$\begin{array}{l} 16 \\ \underline{2/6} \\ 10 \text{ games remain} \end{array}$$

Step (4a)

$$10 \div 3 = 4 \text{ games/day}$$

largest round $= 4$

Answer: Four games per day must be available to run the tournament.

Problem Type III

Example 1

Given: The number of days available to run the tournament (8), and the number of games that can be played per day (4).

What is the maximum number of entries that can be accommodated in the tournament?

Step (1) Determine the appropriate ratio as indicated by the number of games per day (4).

$$\text{appropriate ratio} = 2/6$$

Step (2) Subtract the number of days in the ratio from the days available to find the remaining days. Multiply the remaining days times the games per day to arrive at the remaining number of possible games that can be played.

$$8 - 2 = 6 \text{ remaining days}$$

$$6 \times 4 = 24 \text{ possible games}$$

Step (3) Add the number of games found in step (2) to the number of games in the ratio to arrive at the total games.

$$24 + 6 = 30 \text{ total games}$$

Step (4) Almost two-thirds of the total tournament games occur in the championship bracket. Multiply two-thirds times the total games to find a number which is used as the number of entries in the tournament.

$$\frac{2}{3} \times 30 = 20 \text{ entries}$$

Two checks must be made before accepting the answer.

CHECKS: (1)   games/day $= 4$ largest round $= 8$

no adjustment necessary

(2) Using $N = 20$, determine the number of games in the tournament.

$$\text{number of championship games} = N - 1$$
$$= 20 - 1$$
$$= 19$$

$$\text{number of first-game losers} = \text{first-round games}$$
$$+ \text{second-round games}$$
$$= 4 + 8$$
$$= 12$$

$$\text{number of consolation games} = N - 1$$
$$= 12 - 1$$
$$= 11$$

$$\text{tournament games} = 19 + 11$$
$$= 30$$

This answer (30) equals the number of total games found in step (3). Therefore, no adjustment is necessary.

Answer: Twenty entries can be accommodated in the tournament.

Example 2

Given: Ten days are available to run the tournament, and the available games per day are three.
How many entries can play in the tournament?

Step (1)   Three games per day leads to a ratio of 1/2.

Step (2)

$$10 - 1 = 9 \ \text{remaining days}$$
$$9 \times 3 = 27 \ \text{possible games}$$

Step (3)

$$2 + 27 = 29 \ \text{total games}$$

Step (4)

Round off to higher number.

$$\tfrac{2}{3} \times 29 = 20 \text{ entries}$$

CHECKS: (1) games/day $= 3$ largest round $= 8$

no adjustment necessary

(2) As determined in example 1, the total games for 20 entries is 30. This number is greater than the total possible games (29). The number of entries must be reduced to 19; and it must clear the two checks.

(a) $N = 19$

(b) games/day $= 3$ largest round $= 8$

no adjustment necessary

(c) number of championship games $= N - 1$
$$= 19 - 1$$
$$= 18$$

first-game losers $=$ first-round games
$+$ second-round games
$$= 3 + 8$$
$$= 11$$

number of consolation games $= N - 1$
$$= 11 - 1$$
$$= 10$$

tournament games $= 18 + 10$
$$= 28$$

When a number of entries (whose total games does not exactly match the total possible games) cannot be found, the lower number of entries is accepted as the answer. Therefore, no further adjustment is required.

Answer: Nineteen entries can play in the tournament.

Example 3

Given: The tournament is to be run in five days, and five games can be played per day.

How many entries can play?

Step (1) Five games per day leads to a ratio of 2/6.

Step (2)
$$5 - 2 = 3 \text{ remaining days}$$
$$3 \times 5 = 15 \text{ possible games}$$

Step (3)
$$6 + 15 = 21 \text{ total games}$$

Step (4)
$$\tfrac{2}{3} \times 21 = 14 \text{ entries}$$

CHECKS: (1) games/day = 5   largest round = 6

no adjustment necessary

(2) number of championship games = $N - 1$
$$= 14 - 1$$
$$= 13$$

first-game losers = first-round games + byes
$$= 6 + 2$$
$$= 8$$

consolation games = $N - 1$
$$= 8 - 1$$
$$= 7$$

tournament games = $13 + 7$
$$= 20$$

Try 15 entries.

(a) $N = 15$
(b) games/day = 5   largest round = 7

no adjustment necessary

(c) number of championship games $= N - 1$
$$= 15 - 1$$
$$= 14$$

first-game losers $=$ first-round games $+$ byes
$$= 7 + 1$$
$$= 8$$

consolation games $= N - 1$
$$= 8 - 1$$
$$= 7$$

tournament games $= 14 + 7$
$$= 21$$

Answer: Fifteen entries can play in the tournament.

Example 4

Given: Four days are available to run the tournament, and five games can be played per day.
How many entries can play in the tournament?

Step (1) Five games per day leads to a ratio of 2/6.

Step (2)
$$4 - 2 = 2 \text{ remaining days}$$
$$2 \times 5 = 10 \text{ possible games}$$

Step (3)
$$10 + 6 = 16 \text{ total games}$$

Step (4)
$$2/3 \times 16 = 11 \text{ entries}$$

CHECKS: (1) games/day $= 5$ largest round $= 4$

The games per day must be reduced to four, and the whole process is begun again from step (1).

Step (1a) Four games per day leads to a ratio of 2/6.

Step (2a)
$$4 - 2 = 2 \text{ remaining days}$$
$$2 \times 4 = 8 \text{ possible games}$$

Step (3a)
$$8 + 6 = 14 \text{ total games}$$

Step (4a)
$$\tfrac{2}{3} \times 14 = 10 \text{ entries}$$

CHECKS: (1) games/day $= 4$ largest round $= 4$

no adjustment necessary

(2) championship games $= N - 1$
$$= 10 - 1$$
$$= 9$$

first-game losers $=$ first-round games
$+$ second-round games
$$= 2 + 4$$
$$= 6$$

consolation games $= N - 1$
$$= 6 - 1$$
$$= 5$$

tournament games $= 9 + 5$
$$= 14$$

Answer: Ten entries can play in the tournament.

PROBLEMS FOR SELF-EXAMINATION

(answers in Appendix B)

1. Draw type I consolation tournaments and inject the proper numbers for the following situations:

a. $N = 18$
b. $N = 23$

2. Find the maximum number of games in a type I consolation tournament for the following situations:

a. $N = 7$
b. $N = 35$
c. $N = 20$

3. Set up the rounds of play and games per round for type I consolation tournaments under the following circumstances:

   a. $N = 25$
   b. $N = 17$
   c. $N = 10$

4. Find the minimum number of days required to run a type I consolation tournament under the following conditions:

   a. $N = 17$ and games/day $= 7$
   b. $N = 35$ and games/day $= 3$
   c. $N = 73$ and games/day $= 9$
   d. $N = 43, 13, 25$ and games/day $= 5$

5. Find the minimum number of games that must be played per day in order to run a type I consolation tournament under the following conditions:

   a. $N = 30$ and days $= 10$ b. $N = 13$ and days $= 4$
   c. $N = 58$ and days $= 9$ d. $N = 7$ and days $= 7$

6. Find the maximum number of entries that can be accommodated in a type I consolation tournament under the following conditions:

   a. days $= 4$ and games/day $= 6$
   b. days $= 10$ and games/day $= 2$
   c. days $= 15$ and games/day $= 7$
   d. days $= 11$ and games/day $= 4$

Type II Consolation Tournament

CONSIDERATIONS

Type II consolation is very similar to a double elimination tournament. It consists, however, of two nonconnected brackets. All losers except the final loser of the championship bracket are eventually placed in the consolation bracket.

The winner of the championship bracket is the tournament champion; the winner of the consolation bracket is the third-place finisher. No entry that loses a game has a chance at the regular championship.

The tournament is susceptible to forfeits in the consolation bracket since contestants have no chance at the championship.

Calculations in this section assume that no postponements are possible and that no entry ever plays more than once per day.

Given N, the number of entries in the tournament, the number of games in the tournament can be determined.

Example: $N = 26$

$$\text{number of games} = 2N - 4$$
$$= (2 \times 26) - 4$$
$$= 52 - 4$$
$$= 48$$

Drawing the Bracket

The rules of single elimination draw apply for the construction of the championship bracket. The consolation draw is similar to that for double elimination, except that the last three games of a double elimination tournament are omitted.

N = 14

Championship
Bracket

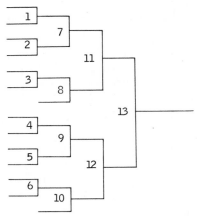

Loser of game 13 does not go to the
consolation bracket, and is considered to
be the second-place finisher.

Consolation
Bracket

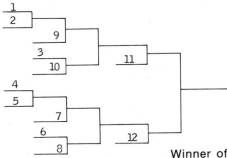

Winner of the consolation bracket is
considered to be the third-place finisher.

TOURNAMENT PROBLEM-SOLVING

Preliminary Considerations

A type II consolation tournament for 32 entries is illustrated on the following pages. As with double elimination, the solutions to type II consolation problems are best understood by working backward.

The chart below describes the relationships between available games per day, ratios, and rounds of play.

GAMES AVAILABLE PER DAY	NUMBER OF DAYS TO PLAY LAST NUMBER OF GAMES	MAXIMUM GAMES FOR EACH ROUND OF PLAY (ROUNDS IN REVERSE ORDER)							
		8	7	6	5	4	3	2	1
2–3	2 days for last 4 games (2/4)							2	2
4–7	4 days for last 12 games (4/12)					4	4	2	2
8–15	6 days for last 28 games (6/28)			8	8	4	4	2	2
16–31	8 days for last 60 games (8/60)	16	16	8	8	4	4	2	2

Rounds of play for tournaments which involve nonperfect rounds are established in the same manner as those for double elimination.

Example: N = 10

Step (1) Determine the number of games in the tournament.

$$\text{number of games} = 2N - 4$$
$$= (2 \times 10) - 4$$
$$= 20 - 4$$
$$= 16$$

Step (2) Select the appropriate ratio—one whose number of games comes closest to the number of games in the tournament without exceeding the tournament games.

$$\text{appropriate ratio} = 4/12$$

N = 32

*Championship
Bracket*

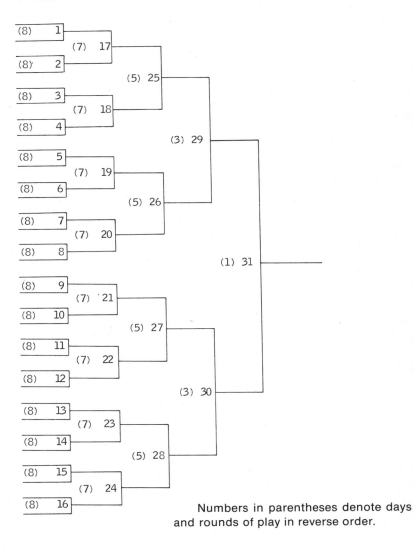

Numbers in parentheses denote days
and rounds of play in reverse order.

N = 32

Consolation
Bracket

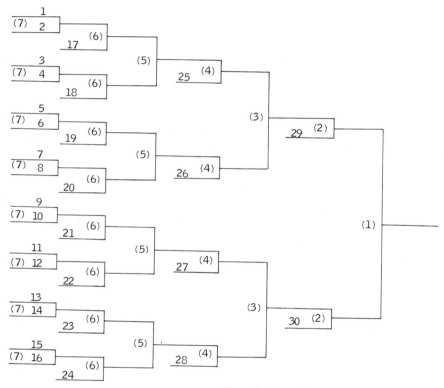

For clarity, all losers are placed in numerical order.

Reminder: The numbers in parentheses, while denoting days of play in reverse order, also indicate rounds of play in reverse order. For purposes of explanation, it is assumed that sufficient games can be played per day so that each round is playable in one day.

Step (3) The ratio immediately establishes the final four rounds of the tournament.

round	4	3	2	1
games	4	4	2	2

Step (4) Subtract games already accounted for (12) from the total number of games in the tournament.

$$16 - 12 = 4 \text{ remaining games}$$

Step (5) If the number of remaining games is equal to or less than the number of games in the last established round (4th to last round in this case), establish the first round of the tournament with that number. However, if the number of remaining games is greater than those in the last established round, the remaining games are divided by two and the first two rounds are established with those numbers.

$$\text{remaining games} = 4$$

$$\text{games in last established round} = 4$$

According to the rule set forth above, the appropriate procedure is to establish the first round with the remaining games (4).

Total sequence of rounds:

round	1	2	3	4	5
games	4	4	4	2	2

$$\text{total games} = 16$$

$$\text{number of rounds} = 5$$

Example: N = 29

Step (1)

$$\begin{aligned}
\text{number of games} &= 2N - 4 \\
&= (2 \times 29) - 4 \\
&= 58 - 4 \\
&= 54
\end{aligned}$$

Step (2) Appropriate ratio = 6/28.

Step (3) The final six rounds are established.

round	6	5	4	3	2	1
games	8	8	4	4	2	2

Step (4)

$$54 - 28 = 26 \text{ remaining games}$$

Since 26 is larger than 8, the appropriate procedure is to divide the remaining games by two and establish the first two rounds.

$$26 \div 2 = 13$$

Total sequence of rounds:

round	1	2	3	4	5	6	7	8
games	13	13	8	8	4	4	2	2

$$\text{total games} = 54$$

$$\text{number of rounds} = 8$$

Problem Type I

Example 1

Given: The number of entries (15), and the number of games that can be played per day (4).
What is the minimum number of days required to run the tournament?

Step (1) Determine the number of games in the tournament.

$$\begin{aligned}
\text{number of games} &= 2N - 4 \\
&= (2 \times 15) - 4 \\
&= 30 - 4 \\
&= 26
\end{aligned}$$

Step (2) Determine the largest round of the tournament. The largest round of a type II consolation tournament is determined as either the first or second round of the championship bracket. Since the championship bracket is a single elimination draw, the numbers of first- and second-round games are found as follows:

$$\text{first-round games} = 15 - 8$$
$$= 7$$

$$\text{second-round games} = 8 \div 2$$
$$= 4$$

$$\text{games/day} = 4 \qquad \text{largest round} = 7$$

$$\text{no adjustment necessary}$$

Step (3) Establish a ratio which corresponds to the games played per day, and subtract the number of games in that ratio from the number of games in the tournament to find the games remaining.

$$\text{appropriate ratio is } 4/12$$

$$26 - 12 = 14 \text{ games remaining}$$

Step (4) Find the days needed to play the remaining number of games by dividing the remaining games by the games played per day. Round off to higher number.

$$14 \div 4 = 4 \text{ days}$$

Step (5) Add the number of days used in the ratio and the days found in step (4) to arrive at the number of days required to run the tournament.

$$4 + 4 = 8 \text{ days}$$

Answer: Eight days are required to run the tournament.

Example 1: N = 15

Championship
 Bracket

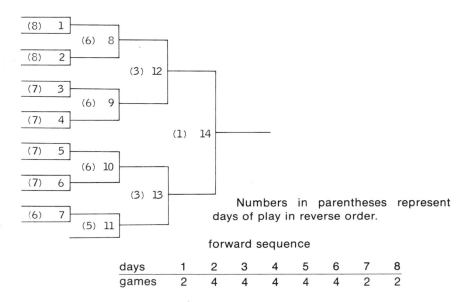

Numbers in parentheses represent days of play in reverse order.

forward sequence

days	1	2	3	4	5	6	7	8
games	2	4	4	4	4	4	2	2

Consolation
 Bracket

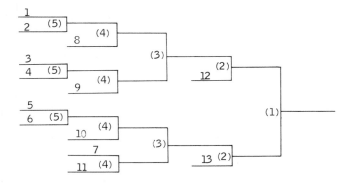

Example 2

Given: Nine entries, and six games can be played per
         day.
What is the number of days needed to run the tournament?

Step (1)

$$\text{number of games} = 2N - 4$$
$$= (2 \times 9) - 4$$
$$= 18 - 4$$
$$= 14$$

Step (2)

$$\text{games/day} = 6 \qquad \text{largest round} = 4$$

The games per day must be reduced to four.

Step (3)   Appropriate ratio is 4/12.

$$14 - 12 = 2 \text{ games remaining}$$

Step (4)
$$2 \div 4 = 1 \text{ day}$$

Step (5)
$$4 + 1 = 5 \text{ days}$$

Answer: Five days are required to run the tournament.

Example 3

Three tournaments are to be run simultaneously.
Given: $N = 10, 17, 25$, and nine games are available for
         play each day.
How many days are required to run the tournaments?

Step (1) Determine the number of games for each tournament.

$$\text{number of games} = 2N - 4$$
$$= (2 \times 10) - 4$$
$$= 20 - 4$$
$$= 16$$

$$\text{number of games} = 2N - 4$$
$$= (2 \times 17) - 4$$
$$= 34 - 4$$
$$= 30$$

$$\text{number of games} = 2N - 4$$
$$= (2 \times 25) - 4$$
$$= 50 - 4$$
$$= 46$$

Step (2) Set up the number of rounds and games for each round of each tournament. Add vertically to get the total number of games for each round.

round	1	2	3	4	5	6	7	8
games ($N = 10$)				4	4	4	2	2
games ($N = 17$)		2	8	8	4	4	2	2
games ($N = 25$)	9	9	8	8	4	4	2	2
total games	9	11	16	20	12	12	6	6

Step (3) With nine games available for play each day, establish the number of days required to play each round.

As with double elimination, days are assigned liberally to avoid the possibility of scheduling entries for play more than once per day.

round	1	2	3	4	5	6	7	8
total games	9	11	16	20	12	12	6	6
				$\dfrac{-2}{18}$				
days		1	2	2	2	2	2	1	1

Answer: Thirteen days are required to run the tournaments.

Problem Type II

Example 1

Given: The number of entries (13), and the number of days available to run the tournament (9).

What is the minimum capability of games played per day necessary to run the tournament?

Step (1) Determine the number of games in the tournament.

$$\text{number of games} = 2N - 4$$
$$= (2 \times 13) - 4$$
$$= 26 - 4$$
$$= 22$$

Step (2) Divide the number of games by the number of days available. This results in an index number which, in turn, indicates the appropriate ratio. When related to ratios, index numbers are considered games per day.

$22 \div 9 = 3$ index number (round off to higher number)

appropriate ratio is 2/4

Step (3) Subtract the number of final games in the ratio from the number of games in the tournament.

$$\begin{array}{r} 22 \\ \underline{2/4} \\ 18 \end{array} \text{ games remaining}$$

Step (4) Two days have been used to play the last four games. Divide the remaining number of days (7) into the remaining number of games (18) to find the required number of games that must be available per day.

$$18 \div 7 = 3 \text{ games/day}$$

This is the correct answer as long as it does not exceed the number of games in the largest round.

$$\text{games/day} = 3 \qquad \text{largest round} = 5$$

Answer: Three games per day must be available to run the tournament.

Example 2

Given: $N = 18$, and six days are available to run the tournament.

What minimum number of games per day is required to run the tournament?

Step (1)
$$\begin{aligned} \text{number of games} &= 2N - 4 \\ &= (2 \times 18) - 4 \\ &= 36 - 4 \\ &= 32 \end{aligned}$$

Step (2)

$$32 \div 6 = 6 \text{ (index number)}$$

appropriate ratio is 4/12

Step (3)

$$32$$
$$\underline{4/12}$$
$$20 \text{ games remaining}$$

$$2 \text{ days remaining}$$

Step (4)

$$20 \div 2 = 10 \text{ games/day}$$

$$\text{games/day} = 10 \qquad \text{largest round} = 8$$

Tournament cannot be run in six days.
Try seven days.

Step (2a)

$$32 \div 7 = 5 \text{ (index number)}$$

appropriate ratio is 4/12

Step (3a)

$$32$$
$$\underline{4/12}$$
$$20 \text{ games remaining}$$

$$3 \text{ days remaining}$$

Step (4a)

$$20 \div 3 = 7 \text{ games/day}$$

$$\text{games/day} = 7 \qquad \text{largest round} = 8$$

Answer: Seven games/day must be available to run the tournament.

Problem Type III

Example 1

Given: The number of days available to run the tournament (10), and the number of games that can be played per day (3).

What is the maximum number of entries that can be accommodated in the tournament?

Step (1) The number of games per day (3) leads to a ratio of 2/4.

Step (2) Two days have been used to play the last four games. Multiply the number of remaining days (8) and multiply them times the available games per day (3) to find the number of possible remaining games.

$$8 \times 3 = 24 \text{ possible games remaining}$$

Step (3) Add the number of remaining games (24) to the number of games in the ratio (4) to find the number of games in the tournament.

$$24 + 4 = 28 \text{ games}$$

Step (4) Inject the number of games (28) into the formula to find N.

$$2N - 4 = 28$$
$$2N = 28 + 4$$
$$N = 32 \div 2$$
$$N = 16$$

Before accepting this as the correct answer, determine the largest round of the tournament and check it against the games per day.

$$\text{games/day} = 3 \qquad \text{largest round} = 8$$

Answer: Sixteen entries can play in the tournament.

Example 2

Given: Seven days are available to run the tournament, and the number of games available per day is nine.

Find the maximum number of entries that can play.

Step (1) Nine games per day leads to a ratio of 6/28.

Step (2) One day remains

$$1 \times 9 = 9 \text{ games remaining}$$

Step (3)
$$28 + 9 = 37 \text{ games}$$
Step (4)

$$2N - 4 = 37$$
$$2N = 37 + 4$$
$$N = 41 \div 2$$
$$N = 20\,{}^{1}\!/_{2}$$
$$N = 20 \text{ (round off to lower number)}$$

games/day $= 9$ largest round $= 8$

Answer is invalid under these circumstances. Reduce the number of games per day until correct solution is found. Try eight games per day.

Step (1) Eight games per day leads to a ratio of 6/28.

Step (2) One day remains

$$1 \times 8 = 8 \text{ games possible}$$

Step (3)
$$28 + 8 = 36 \text{ games}$$

Step (4)

$$2N - 4 = 36$$
$$2N = 36 + 4$$
$$N = 40 \div 2$$
$$N = 20$$

games/day $= 8$ largest round $= 8$

Answer: Twenty entries can play in the tournament.

PROBLEMS FOR SELF-EXAMINATION

(answers in Appendix B)

1. Draw type II consolation tournaments and inject the appropriate numbers for the following situations:

    a. $N = 19$
    b. $N = 24$

2. Set up the rounds of play and games per round for type II consolation tournaments under the following circumstances:

    a. $N = 18$
    b. $N = 27$
    c. $N = 42$

3. Find the minimum number of days required to run a type II consolation tournament under the following conditions:

    a. $N = 45$ and games/day $= 10$
    b. $N = 12$ and games/day $= 4$
    c. $N = 22$ and games/day $= 7$
    d. $N = 9, 29$ and games/day $= 8$

4. Find the minimum number of games that must be played per day in order to run a type II consolation tournament under the following conditions:

    a. $N = 20$ and days $= 7$ b. $N = 29$ and days $= 7$
    c. $N = 40$ and days $= 10$ d. $N = 12$ and days $= 4$

5. Find the maximum number of entries that can be accommodated in a type II consolation tournament under the following conditions:

    a. days $= 5$ and games/day $= 6$
    b. days $= 17$ and games/day $= 4$
    c. days $= 15$ and games/day $= 5$
    d. days $= 20$ and games/day $= 6$

Bagnall-Wild
Consolation Tournament

The purpose of this tournament is to determine realistic second- and third-place finishers. It consists of a championship bracket and at least one, possibly two, consolation brackets.

Example: N = 8

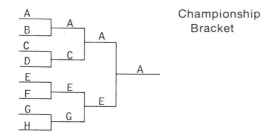

Championship
Bracket

Those entries defeated by the champion compete for second and third places.

2nd Place: B
3rd Place: E

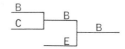

But, if the following occurs,

2nd Place: E

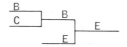

those teams who were defeated by E compete for third place.

3rd Place: F

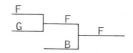

CONSIDERATIONS

The consolation rounds of Bagnall-Wild are of more significance than those of the other consolations discussed; however, the larger the tournament, the longer entries must wait before they know whether or not they are to play again. In the other tournaments, losers were immediately injected into the consolation brackets.

Obvious disadvantages of this type of tournament are that it takes longer to complete than a straight single elimination, and there is no guarantee that every entry plays more than once. Also, forfeits may occur in the consolation rounds since the primary interest of many participants is to win the championship.

The tournament is recommended for use only when dealing with a small number of entries.

Because of the cumbersome nature of this type of tournament, the extent of analysis is very limited.

The calculations in this section assume that no postponements are possible and that no entry ever plays more than once per day.

Given N, the number of entries in the tournament, the following determinations can be made:

1. Maximum Number of Games in the Tournament

Three-round Tournament. Number of games $= N + 3$. When there is only one first-round game, the number of games $= N + 2$.

Four-round Tournament. Number of games $= N + 6$. When only one first-round game, the number of games $= N + 5$.

Five-round Tournament. Number of games $= N + 8$. When only one first-round game, number of games $= N + 7$.

Six-round Tournament. Number of games $= N + 10$. When there is only one first-round game, number of games $= N + 9$.

NOTE: When possible, the loser in the final round of the championship bracket is given a bye in the consolation bracket.

2. Number of Entries in the Consolation Brackets

N^1 represents the number of entries in the first consolation bracket.

N^2 represents the number of entries in the second consolation bracket.

Three-round Tournament. $N^1 = 3$; $N^2 = 3$. When there is only one first-round game, $N^2 = 2$.

Tournaments Greater than Three Rounds. N^1 = number of rounds; N^2 = number of rounds + 1. When only one first-round game, both N^1 and N^2 = number of rounds, or both N^1 and N^2 = number of rounds +1.

DRAWING THE BRACKETS

NOTE: The maximum possibility must always be provided for, so the tournament is drawn with two consolation brackets.

Although the rounds of play are placed in numerical order, the three brackets must be treated as three separate single elimination tournaments for the purposes of problem solving.

> *Reminder:* When possible, the loser in the final round of the championship bracket is given a bye in the consolation bracket.

Example: N = 12

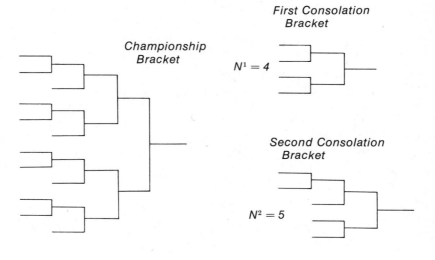

Problem Type I

Example 1

Given: The number of entries (10), and the number of games that can be played per day (3).

How many days are required to run the tournament?

Step (1) The number of rounds in the championship bracket is four, and the games for each round are established as follows:

round	1	2	3	4
games	2	4	2	1

Step (2) Determine the number of entries for the first consolation bracket and set up the number of rounds and games for each round. Add these rounds to those for the championship bracket.

$$N^1 = \text{number of rounds}$$
$$N^1 = 4$$

round	1	2
games	2	1

round	1	2	3	4	5	6
games	2	4	2	1	2	1

Step (3) Determine the number of entries for the second consolation bracket and set up the number of rounds and games for each round. Add these rounds to those already established.

$$N^2 = \text{number of rounds} + 1$$
$$N^2 = 4 + 1$$
$$N^2 = 5$$

round	1	2	3
games	1	2	1

Total sequence:

round	1	2	3	4	5	6	7	8	9
games	2	4	2	1	2	1	1	2	1

Step (4) With three games available for play each day, eliminate as many final rounds as possible. Each bracket is treated as a separate single elimination tournament.

round	1	2	3	4	5	6	7	8	9
games	2	4	2	1	2	1	1	2	1
days			1	1	1	1	1	1	1

Step (5) Start with the first round and work forward.

round	1	2	3	4	5	6	7	8	9
games	2	4	2	1	2	1	1	2	1
		$\dfrac{-1}{3}$							
days	1	1	1	1	1	1	1	1	1

Answer: Nine days are required to run the tournament.

Example 2

Three tournaments are to be run simultaneously.
Given: $N = 15, 6, 18$, and four games can be played per day.
How many days are required to run the tournaments?

Step (1) Set up the number of rounds and games per round for each tournament. Keep the rounds of the three brackets separated.

round	1	2	3	4	5	6	7	8	9	10	11
games ($N = 15$)		7	4	2	1		2	1	1	2	1
games ($N = 6$)			2	2	1		1	1		1	1
games ($N = 18$)	2	8	4	2	1	1	2	1	2	2	1
total games	2	15	10	6	3	1	5	3	3	5	3

Step (2) Establish the number of days required to play each round. Each bracket is treated as a separate single elimination tournament.

round	1	2	3	4	5	6	7	8	9	10	11
total games	2	15	10	6	3	1	5	3	3	5	3
		-2	-3	-1			-3			-1	
		13	7	5			2			4	
days	1	4	2	2	1	1	1	1	1	1	1

Answer: Sixteen days are required to run the tournaments.

PROBLEMS FOR SELF-EXAMINATION

(answers in Appendix B)

1. Draw Bagnall-Wild tournaments for the following situations:

   a. $N = 17$
   b. $N = 28$

2. Find the minimum number of days required to run a Bagnall-Wild tournament under the following conditions:

   a. $N = 21$ and games/day $= 4$
   b. $N = 11$ and games/day $= 5$
   c. $N = 30$ and games/day $= 8$
   d. $N = 7, 25, 18$ and games/day $= 7$

Mueller-Anderson Playback Tournament

The purpose of this tournament is to determine a place ranking for all entries. It consists of a championship bracket and a number of consolation brackets. The concept of the tournament was developed by Pat Mueller and Bruce Anderson, both of the University of Minnesota.

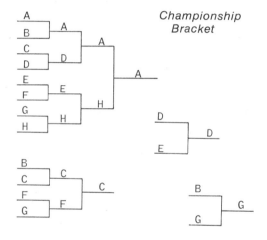

Championship Bracket

Ranking
1st A
2nd H
3rd D
4th E
5th C
6th F
7th G
8th B

CONSIDERATIONS

The disadvantages of running this type of tournament are similar to those for other consolations. Forfeits may occur in the consolation rounds, because the primary interest of many participants is to win the championship. It also requires more games than a single elimination tournament, and it usually requires more days to play.

The method for determining place ranking is not as realistic as that employed in Bagnall-Wild.

There seem to be no formulae for determining the number of games in the tournament or the number of days required to play the tournament. Several listings up to 16 entries have been calculated through counting.

N refers to the number of entries in the tournament; D is the number of days required to play the tournament; and g/d indicates the number of games that can be played per day.

N	Number of Games	N	Number of Games
4	4	11	17
5	5	12	20
6	7	13	22
7	9	14	25
8	12	15	28
9	13	16	32
10	15		

2 g/d		3 g/d		4 g/d		5 g/d	
N	D	N	D	N	D	N	D
4	2	4	2	4	2	4	2
5	3	5	3	5	3	5	3
6	4	6	3	6	3	6	3
7	5	7	3	7	3	7	3
8	6	8	5	8	3	8	3
9	7	9	5	9	4	9	4
10	8	10	5	10	4	10	4
11	9	11	6	11	4	11	4
12	10	12	7	12	5	12	5
13	11	13	8	13	6	13	5
14	13	14	8	14	7	14	5
15	14	15	10	15	7	15	6
16	16	16	11	16	8	16	6

PROBLEM FOR SELF-EXAMINATION

(answer in Appendix B)

1. Draw Mueller-Anderson Playback tournaments for the following situations:

   a. $N = 13$
   b. $N = 26$

Triple Elimination Tournament

CONSIDERATIONS

Triple elimination goes one step beyond double elimination by stipulating that the winner of the tournament is the entry which remains after all other entries lose three contests.

Triple elimination seems most appropriate for a novelty tournament or any situation where one wants to guarantee three contests for every entry.

Triple elimination has an advantage over round robin in that, until eliminated, an entry always has a chance at the championship. An entry in round robin can be eliminated before the schedule is completed. Because of the possibility of premature eliminations, round robin play can lead to forfeits by entries interested only in winning the championship. Forfeits seem less likely with triple elimination.

EXPLANATION

The flow of a triple elimination tournament is somewhat difficult to follow, making its explanation a good mental exercise. A draw for 10 entries appears on the following page and serves as illustration.

Note that the tournament bracket can be seen as three individual single elimination brackets. A loss in the top bracket results in a placement in the middle bracket, and a loss in the middle bracket leads to a drop to the lower bracket. After entry into the final bracket, a subsequent loss eliminates an entry from the tournament.

The numbers in the upper bracket indicate games of play, in sequence. Parenthesized numbers in the middle bracket also represent games of play. Nonparenthesized numbers represent the losers of the corresponding games in the upper bracket. The lower bracket contains numbers that represent the losers of the corresponding games in the middle bracket. Other notations are explained in subsequent paragraphs.

All triple elimination tournaments proceed in the same way until a certain point is reached. That point is at game (9), at which time two general situations can occur. Both are explained in the following contingencies.

Contingency 1

Entry A defeats entry B in game (9) and advances to line Q with no losses. Game (10) is unnecessary and entry B, with two losses, drops to the appropriate slot in the lower bracket. Then, the winner of game R (lower bracket) plays entry A in game I. If entry A wins that game, the tournament is over because all but one entry have three losses. To win the tournament, the survivor of the lower bracket must defeat entry A three times in a row. Game II would be necessary only if entry A lost game I. By the same token, game III would be necessary only if entry A lost a second time. The tournament winner would then be determined by game III.

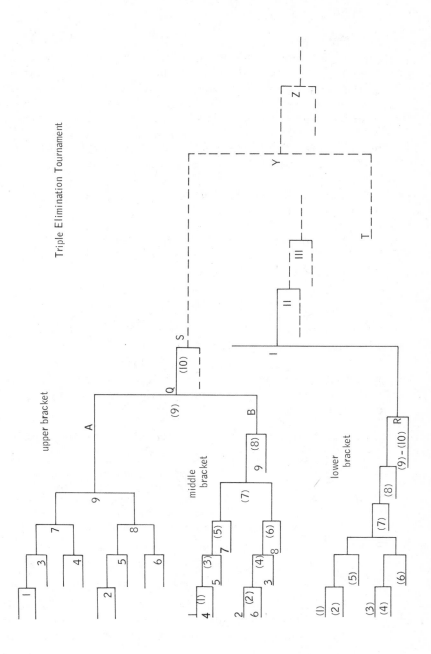

Triple Elimination Tournament

Contingency 2

Entry B defeats entry A, which results in each entry having one loss and makes game (10) necessary. The winner of game (10) advances to line S, and the loser drops to the appropriate line in the lower bracket. The winner of game R (lower bracket) proceeds to line T with two losses. The entries on lines S and T play in game Y. The tournament is over if game Y is won by the entry on line S. Otherwise, game Z would be necessary and would be contended for by entries which have two losses. The winner of game Z is the tournament champion.

Given N, the number of entries in the tournament, the following determinations can be made:

Number of games in tournament $= 3N - 1$

Example: $N = 10$

$$
\begin{aligned}
\text{Number of games} &= 3N - 1 \\
&= (3 \times 10) - 1 \\
&= 30 - 1 \\
&= 29
\end{aligned}
$$

As with double elimination, ratios can be determined to aid in problem solving. The assumption is made that no entry plays more than once per day.

Games Available per Day	Number of Days to Play Last Number of Games
2–3	8 days for last 11 games
4–7	11 days for last 23 games
8–15	14 days for last 47 games

Problem Type I

Given: The number of entries (10) and the number of games that can be played per day (4).

What minimum number of days is needed to run the tournament?

Step (1) Determine the number of games in the tournament.

$$\text{number of games} = 3N - 1$$
$$= (3 \times 10) - 1$$
$$= 29$$

Step (2) Determine the largest round of the tournament. The largest round of a triple elimination tournament is either the first or second round of the upper bracket.

$$\text{largest round} = 4$$
$$\text{games/day} = 4$$

no adjustment necessary

Step (3) Establish a ratio which corresponds to the games played per day, and subtract the number of games in that ratio from the number of games in the tournament to find the games remaining.

With 4 games per day, the appropriate ratio is 11/23.

$$\begin{array}{r} 29 \\ \underline{11/23} \\ 6 \ \text{games remaining} \end{array}$$

Step (4) Find the days needed to play the remaining number of games by dividing the remaining games by the games played per day.

$$6 \div 4 = 2 \ \text{days}$$

Step (5) Add the number of days used in the ratio and the days found in step (4) to arrive at the number of days needed to run the tournament.

$$\text{number of days} = 11 + 2$$
$$= 13$$

Answer: Thirteen days are required to run the tournament.

PROBLEMS FOR SELF-EXAMINATION

(answers in Appendix B)

1. Draw a triple elimination tournament for 17 entries.

2. Find the minimum number of days required to run a triple elimination tournament under the following conditions:

    a. $N = 15$ and games/day $= 5$ b. $N = 7$ and games/day $= 4$
    c. $N = 20$ and games/day $= 7$ d. $N = 35$ and games/day $= 7$

Round Robin
Tournament

CONSIDERATIONS

When leagues are of sufficient size (about 5 entries or more), round robin tournaments require larger numbers of games to complete than any of the other tournaments discussed.

Participation is maximized because each entry is assured of playing every other entry in its league.

The tournament is susceptible to forfeits late in the schedule because entries that have no chance at winning league championships may lose interest.

Round robin is particularly useful for outdoor sports. Rained-out contests need not be played the following day, but may be replayed on the first convenient date. A complete schedule with all dates and times may be printed, therefore, when using round robin leagues.

Given N, the number of entries in a round robin league, the following determinations can be made:

1. Number of games to complete the league schedule $= \dfrac{N(N-1)}{2}$.

Example: $N = 7$

$$\text{number of games} = \frac{N(N-1)}{2}$$

$$= \frac{7(7-1)}{2}$$

$$= \frac{42}{2}$$

$$= 26$$

2. Number of games for each entry $= N - 1$.

Example: $N = 4$

$$\text{number of games per entry} = N - 1$$

$$= 4 - 1$$

$$= 3$$

3. Number of rounds of play in round robin leagues.

$$\text{Even number of entries} = N - 1$$

$$\text{Odd number of entries} = N$$

Examples: $N = 4, 5$

number of rounds $= N - 1$	number of rounds $= N$
$= 4 - 1$	$= 5$
$= 3$	

NOTE: The number of rounds in a league is always odd.

4. Number of games in each round.

$$\text{Even number of entries} = \frac{N}{2}$$

$$\text{Odd number of entries} = \frac{N-1}{2}$$

Examples: $N = 7, 8$

$$\text{number of games/round} = \frac{N-1}{2}$$

$$= \frac{7-1}{2}$$

$$= 3$$

$$\text{number of games/round} = \frac{N}{2}$$

$$= \frac{8}{2}$$

$$= 4$$

ESTABLISHING ROUNDS OF PLAY

Rotation Patterns

Entries are represented by numbers. For all rounds, one digit is held fixed as the other numbers are rotated. For an odd-numbered league, the bye is held fixed. Each pairing represents a game. The rotation, here, is conducted counter-clockwise.

Example: N = 5

		Round		
1	*2*	*3*	*4*	*5*
B–5	B–4	B–3	B–2	B–1
1–4	5–3	4–2	3–1	2–5
2–3	1–2	5–1	4–5	3–4

Example: N = 6

Round				
1	*2*	*3*	*4*	*5*
1–6	1–5	1–4	1–3	1–2
2–5	6–4	5–3	4–2	3–6
3–4	2–3	6–2	5–6	4–5

When the number of entries is even, the top-seeded entries are placed in the top two spots because the (1–2) pairing allows them to play last. For odd-numbered leagues, the final pairing is always (2–N). The top entry is placed in the second spot, and the second seed is placed in the last spot.

Rotation Pattern for a Round Robin between Two Leagues

Example 1

LEAGUE A: 5 entries, represented by Roman numerals.
LEAGUE B: 4 entries, represented by Arabic numerals.

Each entry in league A plays each entry in league B.
When leagues are of unequal size, a bye is placed with those numerals representing the smaller league.
The numerals of one league are held constant while those of the other league are rotated.

Round				
1	*2*	*3*	*4*	*5*
B–I	B–II	B–III	B–IV	B–V
1–II	1–III	1–IV	1–V	1–I
2–III	2–IV	2–V	2–I	2–II
3–IV	3–V	3–I	3–II	3–III
4–V	4–I	4–II	4–III	4–IV

Example 2

LEAGUE A: 5 entries, represented by Roman numerals.
LEAGUE B: 3 entries, represented by Arabic numerals.
In this case, two byes must be placed with the numerals representing the smaller league.

			Round			
	1	*2*	*3*	*4*	*5*
	B–I	B–II	B–III	B–IV	B–V
	B–II	B–III	B–IV	B–V	B–I
	1–III	1–IV	1–V	1–I	1–II
	2–IV	2–V	2–I	2–II	2–III
	3–V	3–I	3–II	3–III	3–IV

In scheduling round robin play, an attempt can be made to assign games to courts or fields in such a manner that each entry plays an equal number of games on each field or court.

There is only one condition under which a perfect relationship can occur. The number of entries must be odd, and the number of courts or fields used must equal the number of games played per round.

Example: $N = 5$, and two courts or fields are available for play.

Horizontal rounds are established, and each entry plays twice on each field or court.

			Round		
Courts or Fields	*1*	*2*	*3*	*4*	*5*
	B–5	B–4	B–3	B–2	B–1
1	1–4	5–3	4–2	3–1	2–5
2	2–3	1–2	5–1	4–5	3–4

Under no other circumstances can all entries be scheduled to play on all courts or fields equally. Close approximations are possible, but there is no easy method for establishing a nearly balanced schedule. Charts for scheduling even-numbered leagues have been established and published by bowling companies. Their use, however, requires that the number of courts or fields equal the number of games played per round.

Partial Round Robin

Each entry plays the same number of games, but no two entries have identical sets of opponents. For extra games, partial round robins can be added to full round robin leagues.

For even-numbered leagues, partial round robins are established by selecting the desired rounds from the rotation patterns. Each round provides one game for each entry.

Example: $N = 14$, and three games for each entry are desired. Any three rounds may be selected, but the first three are illustrated here.

	Round	
1	*2*	*3*
1–14	1–13	1–12
2–13	14–12	13–11
3–12	2–11	14–10
4–11	3–10	2–9
5–10	4–9	3–8
6–9	5–8	4–7
7–8	6–7	5–6

Partial round robins for odd-numbered leagues are established differently. The whole rotation pattern is drawn and rounds of play are established by taking games in horizontal rounds throughout the rotation pattern. Each round of play always provides each entry with two games.

Example: $N = 7$, and four games for each entry are desired.

				Round			
	1	*2*	*3*	*4*	*5*	*6*	*7*
	B–7	B–6	B–5	B–4	B–3	B–2	B–1
	1–6	7–5	6–4	5–3	4–2	3–1	2–7
2	2–5	1–4	7–3	6–2	5–1	4–7	3–6
4	3–4	2–3	1–2	7–1	6–7	5–6	4–5

The first horizontal round provides the following games:

2–5, 1–4, 7–3, 6–2, 5–1, 4–7, 3–6

The second horizontal round provides the following games:

3–4, 2–3, 1–2, 7–1, 6–7, 5–6, 4–5

NOTE: Partial round robins for odd-numbered leagues can only result in an even number of games for each entry.

BLOCK DIAGRAMS

Entries are represented by letters of the alphabet, and rounds are represented by numbers. Procedures for odd- and even-numbered leagues are illustrated.

Example: N = 9

	A	B	C	D	E	F	G	H	I
A	✕	1	2	3	4	5	6	7	8
B		✕	3	4	5	6	7	8	9
C			✕	5	6	7	8	9	1
D				✕	7	8	9	1	2
E					✕	9	1	2	3
F						✕	2	3	4
G							✕	4	5
H								✕	6
I									✕

Step (1) Count across the top line 1 through 8, and down one more in the last vertical column.

Step (2) Count vertically in each column.

Rounds of play are identified by pairing entries connected by the same numbers. Round six, for example, looks like this:

A–G

B–F

C–E

H–I

Example: N = 8

	A	B	C	D	E	F	G	H
A	✕	1	2	3	4	5	6	7
B		✕	3	4	5	6	7	2
C			✕	5	6	7	1	4
D				✕	7	1	2	6
E					✕	2	3	1
F						✕	4	3
G							✕	5
H								✕

Step (1)   Count across the top line 1 through 7.

Step (2)   Count vertically in each column except the last one.

Step (3)   For the last vertical column: Start with 2 and count vertically by twos until the highest round of the tournament is reached.

2–4–6

Stop here because there is no eighth round.

Starting with 1, resume counting by twos.

DOUBLE ROUND ROBIN

Double round robin is established by numbering the second half of the diagram in reverse order.

Example: N = 9

	A	B	C	D	E	F	G	H	I
A	✕	1	2	3	4	5	6	7	8
B	6	✕	3	4	5	6	7	8	9
C	5	4	✕	5	6	7	8	9	1
D	4	3	2	✕	7	8	9	1	2
E	3	2	1	9	✕	9	1	2	3
F	2	1	9	8	7	✕	2	3	4
G	1	9	8	7	6	5	✕	4	5
H	9	8	7	6	5	4	3	✕	6
I	8	7	6	5	4	3	2	1	✕

BLOCK RECORD FORM

	A	B	C	D	E
A		W 3-1	W 2-0	L 0-3	L 2-3
B	L 1-3		W 3-1	L 0-1	W 1-0
C	L 0-2	L 1-3		L 2-4	L 1-2
D	W 3-0	W 1-0	W 4-2		W 2-0
E	W 3-2	L 0-1	W 2-1	L 0-2	

Block record forms can be used to keep league won-lost records.

The form is read horizontally. For example,

> B lost to A, 1–3
> D defeated A, 3–0

Wins and losses are written in different colors for easy reading.

THE STANDINGS

League standings are based on percentages. The first-place entry has the highest winning percentage.

An entry's winning percentage is found by dividing games played into the number of wins.

		W	L
Example:	Pirates	19	5

$$\text{winning } \% = 19 \div 24$$
$$= .791$$

Games behind first place are determined in the following manner.

Example 1

	W	L
Tigers	78	40
Indians	74	45

Step (1)   Find the difference between wins (+4).

Step (2)   Find the difference between losses (+5).

Step (3)   Add the two numbers and divide by two to get the games behind.

$$\text{G.B.} = (4 + 5) \div 2$$
$$= 9 \div 2$$
$$= 4\tfrac{1}{2}$$

Answer: Indians are 4½ games behind the Tigers.

Example 2

	W	L
Yankees	48	57
Orioles	49	62

Step (1)   Difference between wins: −1.

Step (2)   Difference between losses: +5.

Step (3)

$$G.B. = (-1 + 5) \div 2$$
$$= 4 \div 2$$
$$= 2$$

Answer: Orioles are 2 games behind the Yankees.

Complete Standings

	W	L	%	G.B.
Dodgers	63	35	.643	—
Reds	55	42	.567	$7\frac{1}{2}$
Giants	54	43	.557	$8\frac{1}{2}$
Astros	52	48	.520	12
Braves	45	54	.455	$18\frac{1}{2}$

TOURNAMENT PROBLEM-SOLVING

NOTE: Since no entry may play more than once per day, a day's schedule cannot exceed one round for each league.

Problem Type I

Example 1

Given: The number of entries in a league (11), and the maximum number of games that can be played (40).

How many games can be scheduled for each entry?

NOTE: Maximum games are designated by multiplying the number of games that can be played per day times the number of days available to run the tournament.

When working with odd-numbered leagues, horizontal rounds are used just as they are in working with partial round robins.

Step (1)   Divide the number of entries (which is equivalent to the number of games per horizontal round) into the number of games, to find the maximum number of full horizontal rounds that can be played.

$$40 \div 11 = 3 \text{ horizontal rounds}$$

Step (2) Multiply the number of rounds by two to arrive at the number of games.

$$3 \times 2 = 6 \text{ games}$$

Answer: Six games per entry can be scheduled.

Example 2

Given: $N = 8$, and 50 games can be played.
How many games can be scheduled for each entry?

Step (1) Divide the number of entries by two to find the number of games in each round of play.

$$8 \div 2 = 4 \text{ games per round}$$

Step (2) Divide the number of games per round into the maximum number of games to arrive at the number of full rounds that can be played.

$$50 \div 4 = 12 \text{ rounds}$$

Since each entry plays once in every round, the number of games each entry plays equals the number of rounds that can be played.

Answer: Twelve games per entry.

Problem Type II

Given: The number of entries (33), and the maximum number of games that can be played (100).
Divide the entries into the minimum number of possible leagues so that full round robins can be played in each league and a tournament champion can be decided by a single elimination play-off.

Step (1)   Start with one league of 33 entries and determine the number of games required for a round robin.

$$\text{number of games} = \frac{N(N-1)}{2}$$

$$= \frac{33(33-1)}{2}$$

$$= 528$$

A single league results in far too many games, so an estimate is made in splitting the entries into a number of leagues (an effort is always made to achieve homogeneity in league size).

Step (2)   Try three leagues of 7 and two leagues of 6.

$$\text{number of games} = \frac{N(N-1)}{2}$$

$$= \frac{7(7-1)}{2}$$

$$= 21$$

$$\text{number of games} = \frac{N(N-1)}{2}$$

$$= \frac{6(6-1)}{2}$$

$$= 15$$

$21 \times 3 \text{ leagues} = 63 \text{ games} \qquad 15 \times 2 \text{ leagues} = 30 \text{ games}$

$$\text{play-off games} = N - 1$$
$$= 5 - 1$$
$$= 4$$

$$\text{total games} = 63 + 30 + 4$$
$$= 97$$

Answer: Three leagues of 7 and two leagues of 6.

Ancillary Problem

Given: Three leagues of 7 and two leagues of 6.

What is the maximum number of games that can be played per day? (No entry may play more than one per day.)

Step (1)   The problem is solved by adding the number of games in each round of each league.

$$\text{games/round} = \frac{N-1}{2} \qquad\qquad \text{games/round} = \frac{N}{2}$$

$$= \frac{7-1}{2} \qquad\qquad\qquad\quad = \frac{6}{2}$$

$$= 3 \qquad\qquad\qquad\qquad\quad = 3$$

3×3 leagues $= 9$ games $\qquad$ 3×2 leagues $= 6$ games

$$\text{total games} = 9 + 6$$
$$= 15$$

Answer: Fifteen games may be scheduled per day.

Problem Type III

Example 1

Given: The number of entries (21); the league break-down (three leagues of 7); the first day of play (Monday); the days of the week on which regularly scheduled games are played (Monday–Thursday); and the number of games that can be played per day (6).

In how many weeks, and on what day, can the tournament be forecasted to end?

NOTE: The number of days for round robin play cannot be accurately forecasted because of weather delays and league ties that may develop. For purposes of calculation, the following assumptions are made: (1) all postponed games may be completed on weekends, and (2) two days are set aside at the end of league play and are sufficient to cover any possible games resulting from league ties.

Step (1) Determine the maximum number of games that can be played per day, and check that figure against the games available per day. An adjustment must be made if the available games are more than those that can be played.

$$\text{number of games/round} = \frac{N-1}{2}$$

$$= \frac{7-1}{2}$$

$$= 3$$

3×3 leagues $= 9$ maximum games/day

6 games available per day

no adjustment necessary

Step (2) Determine the total number of league games.

$$\text{number of games} = \frac{N(N-1)}{2}$$

$$= \frac{7(7-1)}{2}$$

$$= 21$$

21×3 leagues $= 63$ games

Step (3) Divide the total league games (63) by the number of games available per day (6) to arrive at the number of days required to complete the league schedules. Always round off to higher number.

$$63 \div 6 = 11 \text{ days}$$

NOTE: Answer is correct only if the number of days (11) is not less than the number of rounds (7) in the league with the largest number of entries.

no adjustment necessary

Step (4) Add the number of days set aside for possible games involving league ties (2) and the number of days required to play a single elimination play-off for three league champions (2) to the number of days required to play the league schedules (11).

$$2 + 2 + 11 = 15 \text{ total days}$$

Step (5) Divide the number of tournament days (15) by the number of days scheduled per week (4) to arrive at the number of weeks required to run the tournament.

$$15 \div 4 = 3 \text{ weeks and 3 days}$$

Answer: The tournament should end on the Wednesday of the fourth week.

Example 2

Given: The number of entries (50), the league break-down (two leagues of 9 and four leagues of 8), and the number of games that can be played per day (27).

In how many days can the tournament be played?

Step (1) Determine the maximum number of games that can be played per day, and check it against the games available per day.

$$\text{games/round} = \frac{N-1}{2} \qquad\qquad \text{games/round} = \frac{N}{2}$$

$$= \frac{9-1}{2} \qquad\qquad\qquad\quad = \frac{8}{2}$$

$$= 4 \qquad\qquad\qquad\qquad\quad = 4$$

$$4 \times 2 \text{ leagues} = 8 \text{ games/day} \qquad 4 \times 4 \text{ leagues} = 16 \text{ games/day}$$

$$\text{Total maximum games/day} = 8 + 16$$
$$= 24$$

$$27 \text{ games/day available}$$

Games per day must be reduced to 24.

Step (2)   Determine the total number of league games.

$$\text{number of games} = \frac{N(N-1)}{2}$$

$$= \frac{9(9-1)}{2}$$

$$= 36$$

$$\text{number of games} = \frac{N(N-1)}{2}$$

$$= \frac{8(8-1)}{2}$$

$$= 28$$

$36 \times 2 \text{ leagues} = 72 \text{ games} \qquad 28 \times 4 \text{ leagues} = 112 \text{ games}$

Total league games $= 184$

Step (3)   Divide the total league games (184) by the number of games available per day (24) to arrive at the number of days required to complete the league schedules. Round off to higher number.

$$184 \div 24 = 8 \text{ days}$$

Answer is incorrect because a nine-round league cannot be played in 8 days without having entries play more than once per day. Answer must be adjusted to nine days.

Step (4)   Add the number of days set aside for possible games involving league ties (2) and the number of days required to play a single elimination play-off for six league champions (3) to the number of days required to play the league schedules (9).

$$2 + 3 + 9 = 14 \text{ total days}$$

Answer: Fourteen days are required to complete the tournament.

Problem Type IV

Given: The number of entries (25), the league break-down (three leagues of 6 and one league of 7), and the number of weeks available to run the tournament (5).

What is the minimum number of games that must be available for play each day to complete the tournament?

NOTE: Play starts on a Monday and is scheduled Monday through Thursday.

Step (1) Determine the total number of league games.

$$\text{number of games} = \frac{N(N-1)}{2}$$

$$= \frac{6(6-1)}{2}$$

$$= 15$$

$$\text{number of games} = \frac{N(N-1)}{2}$$

$$= \frac{7(7-1)}{2}$$

$$= 21$$

$$15 \times 3 \text{ leagues} = 45 \text{ games}$$

$$\text{total league games} = 45 + 21$$
$$= 66$$

Step (2) Determine the total number of days available to run the tournament.

$$\text{days} = \text{days/wk.} \times \text{wks.}$$
$$= 4 \times 5$$
$$= 20 \text{ days}$$

Step (3) Two days are set aside for possible games involving league ties, and two days are required to play a single elimination play-off for four league champions. Subtract these days from the total days available to run the tournament.

$$20 - 4 = 16 \text{ days remaining}$$

Step (4) Divide the number of remaining days (16) into the number of league games (66) to find the minimum number of games that must be available per day to run the tournament. Round to higher number.

$$66 \div 16 = 5 \text{ games/day}$$

Answer must be checked against the maximum number of games that can be played per day.

$$\text{games/round} = \frac{N}{2} \qquad \text{games/round} = \frac{N-1}{2}$$

$$= \frac{6}{2} \qquad\qquad = \frac{7-1}{2}$$

$$= 3 \qquad\qquad\qquad = 3$$

$$3 \times 3 \text{ leagues} = 9 \text{ games}$$

$$\text{maximum games/day} = 9 + 3$$
$$= 12$$

Answer: Five games must be available for play each day to run the tournament.

NOTE: The tournament cannot be run unless the number of available days (16) is equal to or greater than the number of rounds (7) in the league with the largest number of entries. That condition is satisfied in this case.

Also, the number of days required to play a single elimination play-off between league winners is considered to be the number of rounds in the play-off. There is only a remote chance that the answer to the problem (games/day) will not be sufficient to cover the play-off in the minimum number of days. Even when that situation occurs, it rarely affects the answer to the problem. For practical purposes, then, the situation requires no further discussion.

Problem Type V

Given: The number of weeks (5) available to run the tournament (20 days, Monday through Thursday), and the number of games that can be played per day (5).

What maximum number of entries can be accommodated in the tournament?

NOTE: Maximum entries can be accommodated when leagues of three entries each are established.

Step (1) Two days are set aside for possible games involving league ties. The number of days required for a single elimination play-off is unknown and must be estimated (6). This estimate may require adjustment as dictated by subsequent solution to the problem. Determine the days remaining for play of league games.

$$\text{days remaining} = \text{days available} - (\text{league ties} + \text{play-offs})$$
$$= 20 - (2 + 6)$$
$$= 20 - 8$$
$$= 12$$

Step (2) Multiply the number of days remaining times the number of games available per day to arrive at the total number of league games that can be played.

$$\text{total league games} = 12 \times 5$$
$$= 60$$

Step (3) Determine the number of games required to complete a round robin schedule for a league of three entries.

$$\text{number of games} = \frac{N(N-1)}{2}$$
$$= \frac{3(3-1)}{2}$$
$$= 3 \text{ games}$$

Step (4) Divide the number of games required to complete a round robin schedule for a league of three entries (3) into the total number of league games available (60) to find the number of leagues that can be accommodated in the tournament.

$$60 \div 3 = 20 \text{ leagues}$$

Step (5) Multiply the number of leagues (20) times the number of entries in each league (3) to arrive at the number of entries that can play in the tournament.

$$20 \times 3 = 60 \text{ entries}$$

Two checks must be made:
  (a) Are six days, as estimated, required to run the single-elimination play-off between 20 league champions?

round	1	2	3	4	5
games	4	8	4	2	1
days	1	2	1	1	1

Six days are, in fact, necessary.

NOTE: If this were not the case, another estimate would be made of days needed to run the play-off and the problem would be worked again.

  (b) Do the games available per day exceed the maximum games that can be played each day?

$$\text{number of games/rd.} = \frac{N-1}{2}$$

$$= \frac{3-1}{2}$$

$$= 1$$

$$1 \times 20 \text{ leagues} = 20 \text{ maximum games/day}$$

This figure is not exceeded by the games available per day (5).

Answer: Sixty entries may be accommodated in the tournament.

PROBLEMS FOR SELF-EXAMINATION

(answers in Appendix B)

1. Assuming no league ties, find the total number of games necessary to play the following round robin tournaments with single elimination play-offs between league winners:

   a. four leagues of 8 teams each
   b. three leagues of 7 teams each and ten leagues of 6 teams each
   c. two leagues of 9 teams each and three leagues of 10 teams each

2. Set up a round robin rotation pattern and a block diagram for 10 entries.

3. Set up a round robin rotation pattern for play between two leagues: league A has 7 entries and is represented by Roman numerals; league B has 8 entries and is represented by Arabic numerals.

4. A round robin league has 9 entries and 10 games of play are desired for each team. Make a listing of league pairings so that the top two seeded teams play each other twice.

5. Determine the winning percentages, games behind, and final standings of the listed teams.

	W	L
Colts	25	40
Stars	35	20
Zeros	62 ·	10
Masons	19	51
Dons	28	27

6. Find the number of games that can be scheduled for each entry in a round robin league under the following conditions:

   a. $N = 7$ and a maximum of 63 games can be played.
   b. $N = 6$ and a maximum of 42 games can be played.

7. Under the conditions stated below, determine the minimum number of possible leagues so that full round robins can be played in each league and a tournament champion can be decided by a single elimination play-off.

   a. $N = 78$ and a maximum of 88 games can be played.
   b. $N = 50$ and a maximum of 100 games can be played.
   c. $N = 29$ and a maximum of 150 games can be played.
   d. $N = 65$ and a maximum of 123 games can be played.

8. Under the conditions stated below, find the number of weeks and the day of the week on which a round robin tournament with single elimination play-off between league champions should end.

   ASSUMPTIONS: Regularly scheduled games are played Monday through Thursday. Postponed games can be completed on weeekends. Two days are set aside at the end of league play to cover the possibility of league ties.

   a. $N = 67$, three leagues of 9 and four leagues of 10, first day of play is a Tuesday, and games played per day is 7.
   b. $N = 35$, five leagues of 7, first day of play is Wednesday, and 8 games can be played per day.
   c. $N = 29$, three leagues of 7 and one league of 8, first day of play is Monday, and 15 games can be played per day.
   d. $N = 45$, nine leagues of 5, first day of play is Thursday, and 5 games can be played per day.

9. Under the listed conditions, find the minimum number of games that must be available for play each day to complete a round robin tournament and single elimination play-off among league winners.

   ASSUMPTIONS: Same as for problem eight.

   a. $N = 37$, three leagues of 7 and two leagues of 8, and 6 weeks are available for play.
   b. $N = 107$, ten leagues of 8 and three leagues of 9, and 9 weeks are available for play.
   c. $N = 43$, two leagues of 8 and three leagues of 9, and 5 weeks are available.
   d. $N = 22$, two leagues of 7 and one league of 8, and 4 weeks are available.

10. Under the listed conditions, find the maximum number of entries that can be accommodated in a round robin tournament and single elimination play-off among league winners.

    ASSUMPTIONS: Same as for problems 7 and 8.

    a. 7 weeks are available and 4 games can be played per day.
    b. 5 weeks are available and 8 games can be played per day.
    c. 10 weeks are available and 3 games can be played per day.
    d. 9 weeks are available and 8 games can be played per day.

SECTION

III

SCHEDULING
AND
EVALUATION

Scheduling

Before the program even begins, the director should have an approximate idea of the sports that are to be in the program, the sequence of their scheduling, and the days of the week and hours of the day on which they will be scheduled. These factors may be affected by so many variables that it is fruitless to try to mention all of them. The availability of facilities, equipment, staff, and officials are a few general items.

At most schools, the availability of facilities for intramural use is dictated by the schedules for classes and varsity practices and games. The intramurals director makes choices based on remaining free time, which usually is comprised of the time before school starts and after school in the late afternoon or evening. The best time for a public school program is immediately after school because of the commuting problem that occurs in the evening. The evening hours are quite good for residential college campuses because the students are available at this time.

If he can, the director should compose a yearly calendar **233** of events for his own office use and also for the publicity of the program. An established program is helpful for both director and participants. Preparations can be made accordingly throughout the year.

ENTRIES

Entries can be taken in two general ways: the participants may fill in and submit an entry form, or the intramural staff can take entries as they come. The latter method is the better of the two, but it involves one distinct problem: someone must be constantly in the office to take entries. If this is not feasible, then certain hours per day may be scheduled as an entry period.

An effort should be made to have the intramural staff take entries, because many disputes and inconveniences can be avoided through direct supervision. Typical problems that arise with the use of entry forms involve situations in which an entry form is submitted and is subsequently misplaced by either the staff or the participant, or a student falsely claims that he has made an entry and there is no satisfactory way to prove that he did not. The basic difficulty with the entry form system is that strict adherence to deadline dates for submission of entries sometimes leads to the unfair elimination of certain entries through errors on the part of the intramural staff. It's a touchy situation when a student who has submitted an entry that has been misplaced comes into the office after a schedule has been drawn up and is upset because he or his team is not on it. The number of such occurrences can be substantially reduced by having the staff take the entries.

Another problem that can be totally eliminated at time of entry is the submission of unacceptable names for independent teams. Names can be changed on the spot; but with the entry form system, team captains must be contacted when the need for change is noted. In addition, the problem of illegible entries can be eliminated at time of entry.

If entry forms are used, specific regulations with respect to legibility and proper disposal of the forms are necessary to avoid later difficulties. Standard information requested on the forms is the sport entered, name, address, phone number of participant, and the organization represented. Added details vary according to sport.

Staff-supervised entries can consist of a simple listing of names, addresses, and phone numbers for each sport, or a more complex set of data can be collected for the larger programs. The basis for taking organization entries is a card-filing system in which all intramural sports are recorded on a set of two or three cards for each organization (Fig. 4). The cards are a quick reference for names and phone numbers and serve as an efficient record-keeping device. The columns to the right of the one for phone numbers are used for records of play (see section on program evaluation).

SCHEDULING

When the entry deadline has passed, all entries are categorized and tabulated. In many established programs, the director knows in advance the types of tournaments he will run for specific sports and divisions. Once the entries are in, he simply constructs the tournament schedules. However, the director of a program whose number of participants varies

ORG. *PHI DELTA THETA*												Year '74	
Sport	Name	Phone	S	P	F	W	MP	EP	TP		IP	TP	
T.F.B.	GEORGE McGURK	8620											
BOWL	GEORGE McGURK	8620											
BASKETBL	HARVY SCHROLL	8620											
SWIM	CHARLIE TOYNER	8413											
VOLLEYBL	BOB EISENBRAUN	2310											
GOLF-T.	KARL STOEDEFALKE	0000											
SOCCER	FRANK SOMMERS	8620											
TRACK	GEORGE McGURK	8620											
TENNIS SING.	1 BILL SIMION	8620											
	2 JOE MANTONE	8413											
GOLF MEDAL	1 CHARLES McCULLOUGH	8620											
	2 MOOSE SWAN	8620											

Figure 4. Entry Card.

substantially from year to year might have to do some quick figuring before deciding on the type of tournament to conduct.

For example, fifteen students enter a badminton tournament. The type of tournament to run depends on any number of factors, but certain alternatives can be established. The numbers of games for the various possibilities are as follows: single elimination, 14; double elimination, 29; and two round robin leagues, 50. The number of days required to complete the tournaments is then calculated by experimenting with different figures for games played per day. A choice might then be based upon the predicted length of the tournaments. Schedule building can begin once these decisions have been made. The procedure for making mimeographed schedules for single elimination, double elimination, and round robin play are described in the following pages.

Single Elimination

An 8×11-inch piece of paper is large enough for charting a tournament for 32 entries. Tournaments for more than 32 entries are divided into flights of 16 or less and are printed on more than one sheet of paper. The procedure for 93 entries is illustrated.

Continually halve the number of entries until all numbers fall between 7 and 17.

93

47–46

24–23–23–23

12–12–12–11–12–11–12–11

The result is eight flights of both 11 and 12 entries. Worksheet brackets are drawn to correspond with the above arrangement, or mimeographed sheets are already available for use. The blank worksheets are arranged in flight sequence, and seeded entries are appropriately placed. The other entries are randomly written on bracket lines. If two entries are from the same organization, they are placed in separate halves of the total bracket so that they do not meet before the finals. Last

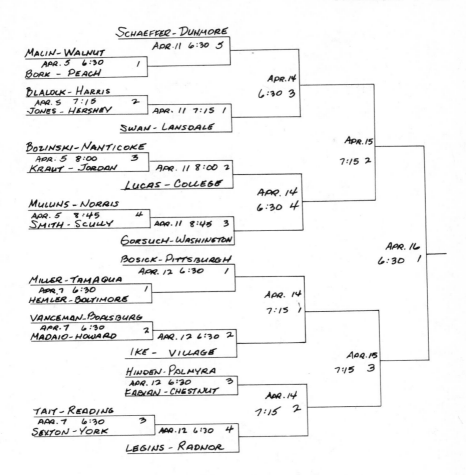

Figure 5. Single Elimination Worksheet.

names and organizations, or organizations alone, are written on each line. Dates, times, and court or field numbers are then written into the bracket (Fig. 5). (Available dates and times should be determined in advance of tournament scheduling.)

When the worksheets are completed, the brackets are drawn on mimeograph stencils with a stencil pen and ruler. Information written on the worksheet is then typed on the stencil. Figure 6 illustrates a finished product.

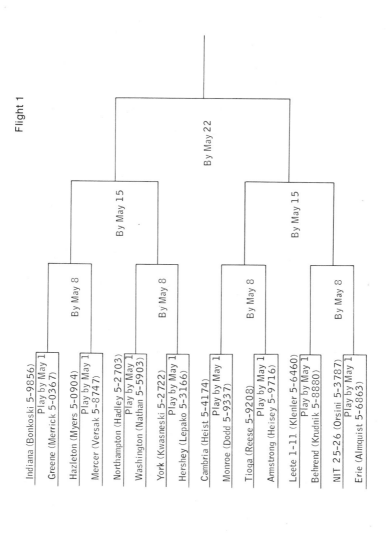

Flight 1

Figure 6. *(Continued on following pages.)*

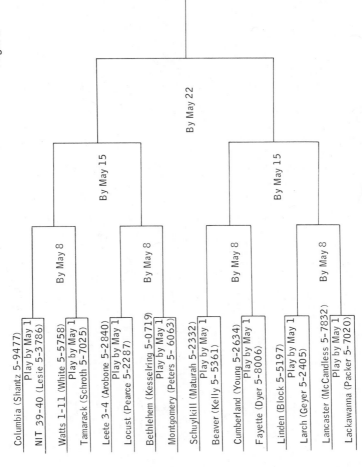

Flight 2

Columbia (Shantz 5-9477)
Play by May 1
NIT 39-40 (Lesie 5-3786)

By May 8

Watts 1-11 (White 5-5758)
Play by May 1
Tamarack (Schroth 5-7025)

By May 15

Leete 3-4 (Arobone 5-2840)
Play by May 1
Locust (Pearce 5-2287)

By May 8

Bethlehem (Kesselring 5-0719)
Play by May 1
Montgomery (Peters 5- 6063)

By May 22

Schuylkill (Maturah 5-2332)
Play by May 1
Beaver (Kelly 5-5361)

By May 8

Cumberland (Young 5-2634)
Play by May 1
Fayette (Dyer 5-8006)

By May 15

Linden (Block 5-5197)
Play by May 1
Larch (Geyer 5-2405)

By May 8

Lancaster (McCandless 5-7832)
Play by May 1
Lackawanna (Packer 5-7020)

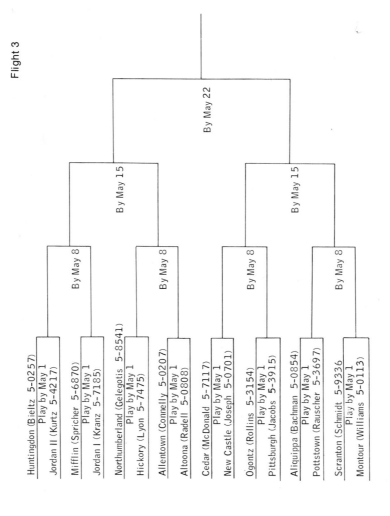

Flight 3

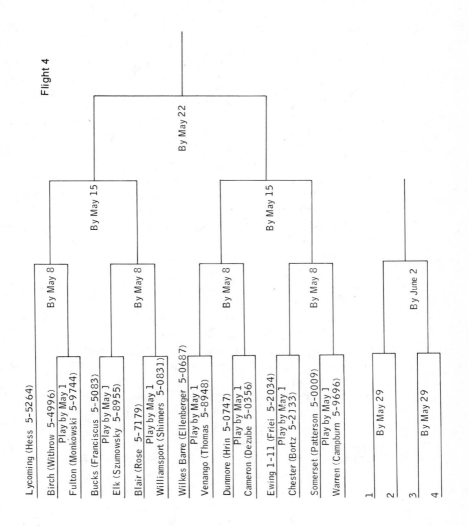

Flight 4

Lycoming (Hess 5-5264)

Birch (Withrow 5-4996)
Play by May 1
Fulton (Monkowski 5-9744)

Bucks (Franciscus 5-5083)
Play by May 1
Elk (Szumowsky 5-8955)

Blair (Rose 5-7179)
Play by May 1
Williamsport (Shinners 5-0831)

Wilkes Barre (Ellenberger 5-0687)
Play by May 1
Venango (Thomas 5-8948)

Dunmore (Hrin 5-0747)
Play by May 1
Cameron (Dezube 5-0356)

Ewing 1-11 (Friei 5-2034)
Play by May 1
Chester (Bortz 5-2133)

Somerset (Patterson 5-0009)
Play by May 1
Warren (Campburn 5-9696)

By May 8

By May 8

By May 8

By May 8

By May 15

By May 15

By May 22

1
2 By May 29
3
4 By May 29

By June 2

Double Elimination

The draw for a double elimination tournament is similar to, but more complicated than, single elimination. A small tournament is illustrated in Figure 7.

Round Robin

Round robin schedules are very easily typed for mimeo-graphing. The procedure for 58 entries follows.

Any number of leagues and league sizes can be drawn for 58 entries. However, the object is to arrive at a number of leagues that permits an equal or nearly equal number of entries in each league. Good league sizes average around eight entries. Dividing eight into 58 entries results in seven with two left over, or five leagues of eight and two leagues of nine.

League rotations for eight and nine entries are either drawn up or are immediately available as worksheets (Fig. 8). For even-numbered leagues, seeded entries are placed at the top of each league. A second round of seeds could be placed in the number-two position so that the one and two teams play each other last. For odd-numbered leagues, seeded entries are placed in the second and last slots. Other entries are filled in at random.

The number of games that can be played per day is kept in mind, and notations are made on the worksheets regarding dates and times of play. Games are alternated between leagues and are scheduled as much as possible to encompass full rounds of play.

The final step is to type out the schedule from the information on the worksheets. Care must be taken to check off on the worksheets the pairings as they are typed. Figure 9 illustrates the first and last pages of a round robin schedule.

When schedules have been mimeographed and stapled and are ready for mailing, it is a good idea to circle or underline in red pencil all matches for each contestant's or team's schedule. This serves three purposes: (1) it helps the participants to readily identify their schedule of games; (2) in the course of underlining, the intramural staff can note any scheduling mistakes or outright omissions of entries; and (3) members of independent teams are reminded of the team names they selected, in case they have forgotten since the time of entry.

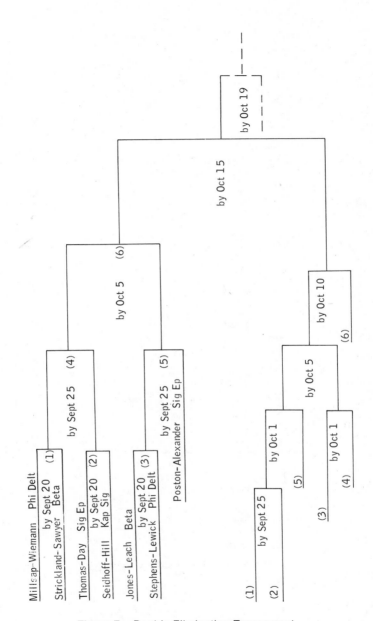

Figure 7. Double Elimination Tournament.

1. Brennan

2. Spoilers

3. Jaspers

4. Kannil

5. SPT

6. All Stars

7. Links

8. Gone

Game	Rotation	Date	Time	Court
1	1-8	2/5	6:30	1
2	2-7	2/5	6:30	2
3	3-6	2/5	6:30	3
4	4-5	2/5	6:30	4
5	1-7	2/12	8:00	1
6	8-6	2/12	8:00	2
7	2-5	2/12	8:00	3
8	3-4	2/12	8:00	4
9	1-6	2/18	6:30	1
10	7-5	2/18	6:30	2
11	8-4	2/18	6:30	3

Figure 8. *(Continued on opposite page.)*

Game	Rotation	Date	Time	Court
12	2-3	2/18	6:30	4
13	1-5	2/25	7:15	1
14	6-4	2/25	7:15	2
15	7-3	2/25	7:15	3
16	8-2	2/25	7:15	4
17	1-4	3/2	7:15	1
18	5-3	3/2	7:15	2
19	6-2	3/2	7:15	3
20	7-8	3/2	7:15	4
21	1-3	3/8	8:30	1
22	4-2	3/8	8:30	2
23	5-8	3/8	8:30	3
24	6-7	3/8	8:30	4
25	1-2	3/19	6:30	1
26	3-8	3/19	6:30	2
27	4-7	3/19	6:30	3
28	5-6	3/19	6:30	4

Figure 9. Round Robin Schedule.

Wichita State University
Intramural Athletics

Frank Rokosz, Director
102 Henrion Gym

UNDERGRADUATE MEN BASKETBALL 1973–74

League A	*League B*	*League C*	*League D*
Beta II	Zarda Brothers	B. B. Jones	Stage Trotters
Beta V	All-Stars	Ind. Ed. Club	Northeast Wichita
Kappa Sig III	Broncos	Dribblers	Wahoos
Sig Ep II	Roofers	Okeefeenokee	Spoilers
SAE III	Brennan I-A	Procrastinators	Beta III
Phi Delt II	Moffitt Heroes	S.P.T.'s	Kappa Sig IV
Phi Delt III	First Floor Nuts	Marauders	Stone Stumblers
Beta IV	A.F. ROTC	Brennan I	Brennan I-B
SAE II	Clutch	MECHA	Beta Donuts
Kappa Sig II			

ALL GAMES PLAYED IN HENRION GYM. MG INDICATES MEN'S GYM.
WG INDICATES WOMEN'S GYM.

Lg.					
A	BETA II VS KAPPA SIG II	Tues. Oct. 30		8:45	MG
A	BETA V VS SAE II	" " "		8:45	WG
A	KAPPA SIG III VS BETA IV	Wed. Oct. 31		6:30	MG
A	SIG EP II VS PHI DELT III	" " "		7:15	MG
A	SAE III VS PHI DELT II	" " "		8:00	MG
B	ZARDA BROTHERS VS A.F. ROTC	" " "		8:45	MG
B	ALL-STARS VS FIRST FLOOR NUTS	" " "		6:30	WG
B	BRONCOS VS MOFFITT HEROES	" " "		7:15	WG
B	ROOFERS VS BRENNAN I-A	" " "		8:00	WG
C	B.B. JONES VS BRENNAN I	" " "		8:45	WG
B	CLUTCH VS FIRST FLOOR NUTS	Mon. Nov. 5		8:00	WG
B	ZARDA BROTHERS VS MOFFITT HEROES	" " "		8:45	WG
C	IND. ED. CLUB VS MARAUDERS	" " "		8:00	MG
C	DRIBBLERS VS S.P.T.'s	" " "		8:45	MG
C	OKEEFEENOKEE VS PROCRASTINATORS	" " "		6:30	WG
D	STAGE TROTTERS VS BRENNAN I-B	" " "		6:30	MG
D	NORTHEAST WICHITA VS STONE STUMB.	" " "		7:15	MG

Figure 9. (*Continued on opposite page.*)

Lg.

A	BETA II VS SAE II	Tues. Nov. 6	8:00	MG
A	KAPPA SIG II VS BETA IV	" " "	8:45	MG
A	BETA V VS PHI DELT III	" " "	6:30	WG
A	KAPPA SIG III VS PHI DELT II	" " "	7:15	WG
A	SIG EP II VS SAE III	" " "	8:00	WG
B	ALL-STARS VS BRENNAN I-A	" " "	8:45	WG
D	WAHOOS VS KAPPA SIG IV	" " "	6:30	MG
D	SPOILERS VS BETA III	" " "	7:15	MG
B	ALL-STARS VS CLUTCH	Mon. Feb. 4	6:30	WG
B	BRONCOS VS A.F. ROTC	" " "	7:15	WG
B	ROOFERS VS FIRST FLOOR NUTS	" " "	8:00	WG
B	BRENNAN I-A VS MOFFITT HEROES	" " "	8:45	WG
C	IND. ED. CLUB VS MECHA	" " "	6:30	MG
C	DRIBBLERS VS BRENNAN I	" " "	7:15	MG
C	OKEEFEENOKEE VS MARAUDERS	" " "	8:00	MG
C	PROCRASTINATORS VS S.P.T.'s	" " "	8:45	MG
A	PHI DELT II VS SAE II	Wed. Feb. 6	6:30	WG
A	PHI DELT III VS BETA IV	" " "	7:15	WG
A	BETA II VS BETA V	" " "	8:00	WG
D	WAHOOS VS STAGE TROTTERS	" " "	6:30	MG
D	SPOILERS VS BETA DONUTS	" " "	7:15	MG
D	BETA III VS BRENNAN I-B	" " "	8:00	MG
D	KAPPA SIG IV VS STONE STUMBLERS	" " "	8:45	MG
A	KAPPA SIG III VS KAPPA SIG II	Tues. Feb. 12	6:30	WG
A	SIG EP II VS SAE II	" " "	7:15	WG
A	SAE III VS BETA IV	" " "	8:00	WG
A	PHI DELT II VS PHI DELT III	" " "	8:45	WG
D	NORTHEAST WICHITA	Wed. Feb. 13	6:30	MG
D	WAHOOS VS BRENNAN I-B	" " "	7:15	MG
D	SPOILERS VS STONE STUMBLERS	" " "	8:00	MG
D	BETA III VS KAPPA SIG IV	" " "	8:45	MG

A

B

C

D

MASTER SCHEDULES

Especially in larger programs containing several divisions of play (dormitory, fraternity, independent, women, and so forth), the director may want to establish a master schedule worksheet showing the divisions and, perhaps, the leagues that are playing each day. Without a master schedule, the question of who is playing on any particular day can be answered only by rummaging through all the schedules. The master schedule allows one to identify the correct division quickly, then the proper schedule can be examined.

Master schedules for divisions of round robin leagues require a simple coding system of two letters—one for the division and one for the league. For example, I-B indicates league B of the independent division. The numbers represent the number of games for each league.

MASTER SCHEDULE

Date	6:30	7:30	8:30
Thurs. 2/8	4 I-A	2 F-C 2 D-C	4 W-A
Mon. 2/12	1 W-C 3 D-F	4 D-A	4 I-C
Tues. 2/13	4 W-B	2 F-C 2 D-C	2 I-B 2 F-D
Wed. 2/14	4 D-B	1 D-F 3 W-C	4 I-A
Thurs. 2/15	2 W-A 2 I-C	4 D-E	4 F-D

PRECAUTIONS

Always provide for league ties and postponed games in tournaments where they can occur. Postponed games can probably be played on weekends, but one does not want to get worked into a corner at the end of the schedule. A few days at the end should be left open.

Participants should not be overscheduled. One or two games per week is sufficient. Overscheduling is particularly tempting in programs for which small numbers of entries are the rule. Small tournaments can be run quickly, but participants can't be expected to play every night. A possible solution is to run two or more small tournaments simultaneously and to alternate days of play.

The director must never outschedule his supply of officials for contests. Even if an unlimited number of courts or fields were available, the number of available officials would limit play. About three times as many officials should be available as are needed per day. If 15 officials must be scheduled per day, then the total corps of officials should be about 45.

PROBLEMS FOR CONSIDERATION

(no answers in Appendix)

1. What types of tournaments can be run under the following conditions?
   ASSUMPTIONS: Play is Monday through Thursday. Postponed games can be played on weekends.

   a. $N = 39$, games/day $= 6$, and no more than 5 weeks can be allowed for play.
   b. $N = 84$, games/day $= 8$, and no more than 4 weeks are available for play.
   c. $N = 17$, games/day $= 4$, and no more than 3 weeks are available for play.

2. Under the listed conditions, compare three tournaments (single elimination, double elimination, and round robin) with respect to the minimum number of games that must be played per day to complete the tournaments.

   a. $N = 35$ (five leagues of 7) and days $= 8$
   b. $N = 20$ (four leagues of 5) and days $= 10$
   c. $N = 83$ (seven leagues of 8 and three leagues of 9) and days $= 26$.

3. For each number of entries in a round robin tournament, find several combinations of league breakdowns without having the number of entries in each league differ by more than one. Determine the number of games for each combination.

   a. $N = 28$ b. $N = 98$ c. $N = 61$ d. $N = 75$

4. Under the conditions listed below, compare three tournaments (single elimination, type I consolation, and type II consolation) with respect to the maximum number of entries that can be accommodated in the tournaments.

   a. days = 26 and games/day = 3
   b. days = 15 and games/day = 5
   c. days = 20 and games/day = 8

17

Program Evaluation

Intramurals is a numbers game. Programs can be evaluated in a variety of subjective ways, but the most effective means is through intramurals statistics. In terms of acquiring funds and facilities, all the flowery statements about the need for intramurals and the success of a particular program are not nearly as valuable as solid participation figures. In addition, proper interpretation of intramurals statistics can indicate the good and bad points of a program and alert one to necessary adjustments. Statistics also serve as predictors for what is to come in following years. Every effort, then, should be made to keep accurate and meaningful records.

RECORD-KEEPING DURING SPORT SEASONS

Scoresheets play an important role in intramural programs. They are the grass roots of record-keeping. Scoresheets should be kept compact and simple so that officials can easily handle the task of scoring contests.

DATE __1/24__ TIME __7:15__ COURT __3__

TEAM _ALL STARS_	TM. OUT 1 2	TEAM _JASPERS_	TM. OUT 1 2
JACKSON	p.f. ① 2 3 4 5	_MILETICH_	p.f. ① 2 3 4 5
ALLISON	p.f. ①② 3 4 5	_CASEY_	p.f. 1 2 3 4 5
BARTER	p.f. 1 2 3 4 5	_MILLS_	p.f. 1 2 3 4 5
HAROLDSON	p.f. 1 2 3 4 5	_SHOEMAN_	p.f. ①②③ 4 5
CARVER	p.f. 1 2 3 4 5	_VAUGHN_	p.f. 1 2 3 4 5
BLACK	p.f. ① 2 3 4 5	_STEVENS_	p.f. 1 2 3 4 5
JURGENSON	p.f. 1 2 3 4 5		p.f. 1 2 3 4 5
	p.f. 1 2 3 4 5		p.f. 1 2 3 4 5
	p.f. 1 2 3 4 5		p.f. 1 2 3 4 5
	p.f. 1 2 3 4 5		p.f. 1 2 3 4 5
	p.f. 1 2 3 4 5		p.f. 1 2 3 4 5
	p.f. 1 2 3 4 5		p.f. 1 2 3 4 5
	p.f. 1 2 3 4 5		p.f. 1 2 3 4 5

John Miletich

24

1	2	3	4	5	6	7	8	9	10	11	12	13	14	15	16
17	18	19	20	21	22	23	24	25	26	27	28	29
30	31	32	33	34	35	36	37	38	39	40	41	42
43	44	45	46	47	48	49	50	51	52	53	54	55
56	57	58	59	60	61	62	63	64	65	66	67	68
69	70	71	72	73	74	75	76	77	78	79	80	81

35

1	2	3	4	5	6	7	8	9	10	11	12	13	14	15	16
17	18	19	20	21	22	23	24	25	26	27	28	29
30	31	32	33	34	35	36	37	38	39	40	41	42
43	44	45	46	47	48	49	50	51	52	53	54	55
56	57	58	59	60	61	62	63	64	65	66	67	68
69	70	71	72	73	74	75	76	77	78	79	80	81

Figure 10.

A sample basketball scoresheet (Fig. 10) provides space for a listing of players, running score, and times out. It is a good precautionary measure to have winning captains sign the scoresheet after the game. Every once in a while a scorekeeper will inadvertently reverse scores and indicate the losing team as the winner. The signature of the winning captain almost surely indicates the winning team. Very rarely, if ever, will the losing captain sign the scoresheet, either intentionally or unintentionally.

For round robin play, scores are recorded in league block forms (Fig. 11). Each score is recorded twice—once for each team. Wins are written in blue and losses in red for easy reading. The form is read from left to right. Figure 11 shows that the All Stars lost to the Jaspers by 1–3, and the Cariocas beat the Aces by 1–0. (The columns on the right side of the form are explained later in this chapter.)

Names of players are taken from the scoresheet and listed on the participation sheet for each team (Fig. 12). New names are added from game to game, and repeated names are checked under the appropriate dates. This serves as the team roster during the course of the season. At the end of a team's season, two figures are compiled — individual participation (the number of players who played at least one game) and total participation (the collective number of participations by all players, i.e., the number of marks on the sheet).

The statistics for individual participation often are misleading because its definition is not standardized. A track and field meet, for instance, has several events within the sport. Individual participation should be recorded in such a way as to avoid counting a contestant more than once even though he may participate in more than one event. For example, one

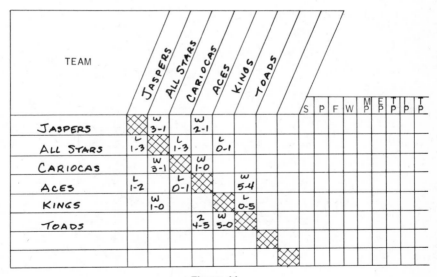

LEAGUE _B_

Figure 11.

PAYROLL or PARTICIPATION

CHARGERS

	1/24	1/25	1/26	1/30													
HALSEY	/	/	/	/													
KINARD	/	/	/	/													
AINSLEY	/		/	/													
WHITING	/	/															
FISHER	/	/	/	/													
SMITHON	/	/		/													
HASKELL	/		/														
MASON		/															
MACK		/	/														
HANSAN		/															
FIFE		/															
BAIR			/														
CHISHAM			/														

Figure 12.

occasionally sees instances in which individual participation for the 100-yard dash is added to that for the 220-yard dash. This procedure results in an inflated figure for individual participation because certain repetitions are involved. Jim Jones, who participated in the 100-yard dash, the 220-yard dash, and the mile run, is counted three times instead of once. Frequently, individual participation figures for all sports are added for an end-of-the-year summary. Again, such a total does not indicate true individual participation, because of multiple participation by certain students. Many students participate in more than one sport during the course of the year. A true individual participation statistic for the year is difficult to compile, because it involves the keeping of master lists of student participation across all sports — a time-consuming and potentially inaccurate task. A standard procedure is to maintain a filing system that contains an index card for every participant. Each participant is listed on a separate card, which is alphabetically listed in the system. As the year proceeds, only new intramural participants are injected into the filing system. At the end of the year, the cards are counted to arrive at the number of students and faculty who participated in the intramural program at least once during the year. From this figure, the percentage of the institutional community that participated in intramurals at any time during the year can be calculated.

Progress of elimination tournaments is penciled on the schedule with names and scores appropriately assigned (Fig. 13).

FINAL SPORT SUMMARY

At the conclusion of each sport season, a small packet of statistical information is compiled to form the final sport summary. It consists of a cover sheet (Fig. 14), a number of summary sheets (one for each division of play) (Fig. 15), and any schedules and play-off draws that were employed in the tournament. Round robin schedules are attached as printed, but the progress of all elimination schedules and play-offs are typed onto the schedules.

Development of sport summaries for round robin, single and double elimination, and meet tournaments is described in the following pages.

Wichita State University
Intramural Athletics
Undergraduate Men's Tennis 1973

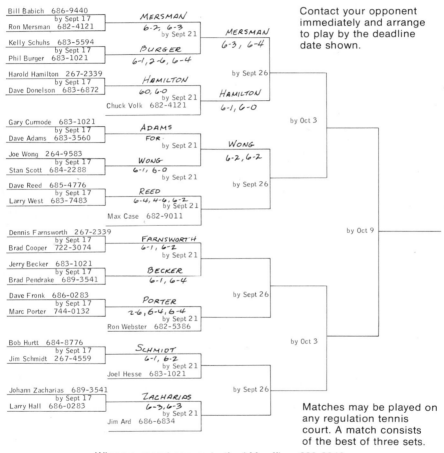

Contact your opponent
immediately and arrange
to play by the deadline
date shown.

Matches may be played on
any regulation tennis
court. A match consists
of the best of three sets.

Winners report scores to the I.M. office, 689-3340.

Figure 13. Single Elimination Progress.

WICHITA STATE UNIVERSITY
INTRAMURAL ATHLETICS
ACTIVITY SUMMARY SHEET

Division	Season	Type Tour	Entries	Contests Sched	Contests Played	Per cent Played	Indiv. Part.	Total Part.
Ungrad Men								
Ungrad Women								
Grad-Fac Men								
Grad-Fac Women								
Fraternity								
Totals								

Division	Champion
Ungrad Men	—
Ungrad Women	—
Grad-Fac Men	—
Grad-Fac Women	—
Fraternity	—

Comparison with Last Year

			Inc.-Dec.	Per cent Inc.-Dec.
Entries				
Contests Scheduled				
Contests Played				
Per cent Played				
Indiv. Participation				
Total Participation				

Notes:

Figure 14. Cover Sheet.

ENTRY	SCHED	PLAY FOR	WIN	IP	TP	PLACE POINTS

Figure 15.

Round Robin Statistics

Compilation of round robin statistics begins with a block record form. Three small block forms appear in Figure 16 and serve to illustrate three different statistical situations. All three forms involve the records of four-team leagues. Each team's wins and losses have been recorded on the form, and final league records appear on the right-hand side. The letters above the columns indicate the following: S = scheduled games, P = played games, F = forfeits, and W = wins. These

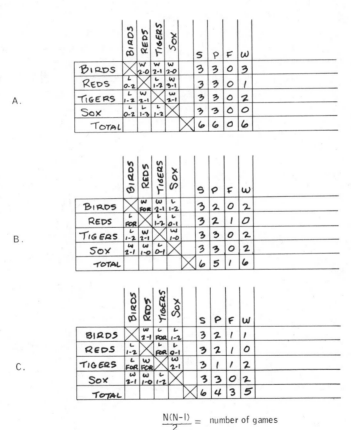

$$\frac{N(N-1)}{2} = \text{number of games}$$

Figure 16. Three League Block Forms.

are not the only statistics that would appear on a larger league block form, but they are the only ones necessary to the understanding of statistical computation.

Totals for each category appear on the bottom line of each form. Note that in the top form, for example, the totals for the columns scheduled and played are one-half of what they apparently should be. The arithmetical total of each of those columns is divided by two in order to get the real total, because each game played in the league was recorded twice on the block form (once for each team).

When the totals have been compiled, they must be checked against three relationships to verify their accuracy. Form A represents the situation in which all games were played and no forfeits occurred.

Relationship I: The total for scheduled games must be checked with the formula for the number of games in a round robin tournament, which appears at the bottom of Figure 16 and looks like this when the figures are injected:

$$\frac{4(4-1)}{2} = 6$$

Relationship I is accurate; the formula total and the arithmetical total both equal six.

Relationship II: The scheduled games minus the played games must equal the number of forfeits.

$$S - P = F$$
$$6 - 6 = 0$$

Relationship II is accurate; zero equals zero.

Relationship III: The number of wins must equal the number of scheduled games.

$$\text{wins} = \text{games}$$
$$6 = 6$$

Relationship III is satisfied.

The statistics are accurate when all three relationships are satisfied. Should one or more relationships be out of balance, the statistical error must be found by rechecking calculations.

Form *B* describes a situation in which one or more forfeits are present. The Birds defeated the Reds by forfeit, and the Reds lost to the Birds by forfeit. As illustrated, neither team is credited with a played game for a forfeited contest. The totals are compiled as explained earlier. The relationships must be checked again. It can be quickly determined that the arithmetical total of six scheduled games equals the formula total of six. Relationship II is satisfied because scheduled games minus played games $(6 - 5 = 1)$ equals the number of forfeits (1). As before, the number of wins (6) equals the number of scheduled games (6), so relationship III is satisfied also.

In Form *C* a double forfeit has occurred. The Birds lost to the Tigers by forfeit, and the Tigers lost to the Birds by forfeit. As in the first two cases, relationship I is satisfied. Relationship II is a different story, though. Scheduled games minus played games $(6 - 4 = 2)$ does not equal the number of forfeits (3). This is to be expected, however, when a double forfeit exists. Normally, a forfeited game involves a forfeit by only one of the two teams scheduled. When a double forfeit occurs, both teams are credited with forfeits; thus the extra forfeit. Relationship III is not satisfied either; the number of wins (5) does not equal the number of scheduled games (6). However, that also is to be expected in a double forfeit situation, because neither team that forfeited can be credited with a win. Therefore, each double forfeit results in a situation in which one can expect one more forfeit than normal and one less win than normal.

A completed league block form is illustrated in Figure 17. Starting with the fifth column from the left, the letters refer to the following: MP = match points, EP = entry points, TP = total points, IP = individual participation, and TP = total participation. The figures for MP, EP, and TP are awarded through the point system for an all-year trophy.

After all leagues have checked out statistically, each entry of each league is placed on a divisional summary sheet (Fig. 18). Any play-off action across leagues is reflected in the individual records of the entries. The same rules apply to the totals for the summary sheet as for the league block forms.

When all summary sheets are completed and checked,

LEAGUE ___C___

TEAM	KANINES	COLTS	HIJACKERS	HITTERS	CHEETAHS					S	P	F	W	M P	E P	T P	T P	T P
KANINES		W 16-13	W 15-14	W 7-5	W 10-1					4	4	0	4	40	25	65	13	41
COLTS	L 13-16		L FOR	W 10-9	L 3-7					4	3	1	1	10	0	10	16	36
HIJACKERS	L 14-15	W FOR		W 20-5	W 9-2					4	3	0	3	30	25	55	14	35
HITTERS	L 5-7	L 9-10	L 5-20		L 6-10					4	4	0	0	0	25	25	14	33
CHEETAHS	L 1-10	L 7-3	L 2-9	W 10-5						4	4	0	2	20	25	45	12	40
										10	9	1	10				69	185

Figure 17.

the totals are transferred to the cover sheet (Fig. 19). The completed packet then consists of the cover sheet, the appropriate number of summary sheets, and the round robin schedules.

Single Elimination Statistics

Whereas round robin statistics are transferred from scoresheet to league block form to summary sheet, the figures for single elimination play are taken directly from the bracket and placed on the summary sheet. Three different statistical examples are illustrated in Figure 20. On the left-hand side of the page, three completed progressions of single elimination play appear, and the number of entries is seven. Compact versions of the divisional summary sheet appear to the right of each bracket.

The record of play for each entry is tabulated on the summary sheet. In the top bracket, entry A, for example, lost to entry B (1–2) in the first game. Entry A's record is appropri-

Dormitory Division

Entry	Sched	Play	For	Win	IP	TP	Place	Points	
Harvard	5	5	0	3	25	88		55	
Yale	6	6	0	4	30	52		125	
Princeton	4	4	0	1	22	75		35	
Cornell	4	4	0	0	25	65		25	
Rutgers	6	6	0	5	13	61	1	200	
Penn State	6	6	0	4	25	61	2	165	
Pitt	4	4	0	0	30	74		25	
Ohio State	4	4	0	1	22	50		35	
Indiana	6	6	0	4	17	47		125	
Mississippi	5	5	0	3	23	49		55	
Total	25	25	0	25	232	622			

Figure 18.

Wichita State University
Intramural Athletics

Basketball 1973–74

Division	Season	Type Tour	Entries	Contests Sched	Contests Played	Per cent Played	Indiv. Part.	Total Part.
Ungrad Men	Oct 30 - Mar 5	R. R.	37	157	110	70	477	1726
Ungrad Women	Oct 30 - Feb 13	R. R.	6	30	22	73.3	93	372
Grad-Fac Men	Nov 3 - Feb 28	R. R.	5	21	19	90	63	268
Grad-Fac Women								
Fraternity	Nov 3 - Mar 5	R. R.	7	42	37	88.1	106	539
Totals			55	251	189	75.3	739	2905

Division	Champion
Ungrad Men	Roofers
Ungrad Women	Grace Wilkie
Grad-Fac Men	Minority Studies
Grad-Fac Women	
Fraternity	Phi Delta Theta

Comparison with Last Year	72-73	73-74	Inc.-Dec.	Per cent Inc.-Dec.
Entries	52	55	+3	+5.4
Contests Scheduled	230	251	+21	+8.3
Contests Played	168	189	+21	+11.1
Per cent Played	73.0	75.3	+2.3	+3.0
Indiv. Participation	672	739	+67	+9.1
Total Participation	2813	2905	+92	+3.2

Notes: One University Championship Game Added.

Figure 19.

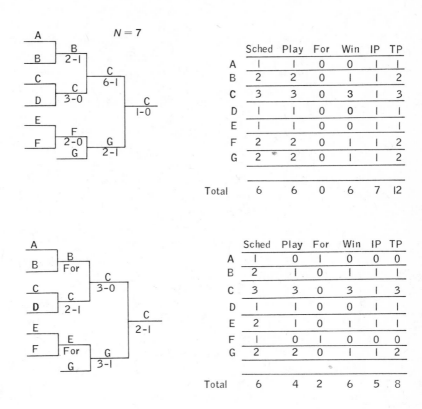

	Sched	Play	For	Win	IP	TP
A	1	1	0	0	1	1
B	2	2	0	1	1	2
C	3	3	0	3	1	3
D	1	1	0	0	1	1
E	1	1	0	0	1	1
F	2	2	0	1	1	2
G	2	2	0	1	1	2
Total	6	6	0	6	7	12

	Sched	Play	For	Win	IP	TP
A	1	0	1	0	0	0
B	2	1	0	1	1	1
C	3	3	0	3	1	3
D	1	1	0	0	1	1
E	2	1	0	1	1	1
F	1	0	1	0	0	0
G	2	2	0	1	1	2
Total	6	4	2	6	5	8

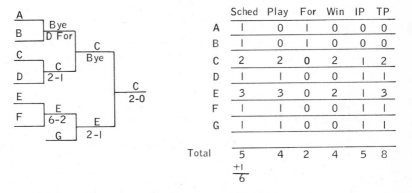

	Sched	Play	For	Win	IP	TP
A	1	0	1	0	0	0
B	1	0	1	0	0	0
C	2	2	0	2	1	2
D	1	1	0	0	1	1
E	3	3	0	2	1	3
F	1	1	0	0	1	1
G	1	1	0	0	1	1
Total	5 +1 / 6	4	2	4	5	8

Figure 20. Three single elimination brackets and summaries.

ately assigned to the summary sheet, as are all the records for all the entries. The totals are calculated in the same manner as were those for round robin. The scheduled and played arithmetical totals must be halved in order to get the true number of games scheduled and played.

The same relationships that were used to check the accuracy of round robin totals are employed for single elimination. Relationship I, which checks the arithmetical total of scheduled games against the formula ($N - 1 =$ games) total, checks out because both equal six games. Relationship II ($S - P = F$) is satisfied since both sides of the equation equal zero. Relationship III ($S = W$) checks out too, because both sides of the equation equal six.

The middle bracket and summary illustrate the situation in which forfeits are involved. It can be readily determined that all three relationships are on balance.

The bottom bracket and summary involve a double forfeit. In the first game, A and B double-forfeit to create a bye in the second round. Entry C is advanced to the final round because of the bye. Entry C cannot be credited with a game scheduled, played, or won in round two. Neither A nor B can be credited with winning the first game. These factors are reflected in the summary totals. The arithmetical total of scheduled games (5) does not equal the formula total of six, but that is to be expected since an unscheduled bye occurred in round two. One game is added to the arithmetical total to account for all the originally scheduled games. When the other two relationships are checked, the arithmetical total for scheduled games (5) is used. A look at the two relationships shows the existence of one more forfeit than normal and one less win than normal. That is appropriate for each double forfeit.

The final packet is formed as it was with round robin, except that the attached schedules have the tournament progressions typed on them.

Double Elimination Statistics

Double elimination statistics are handled in approximately the same manner as were those for single elimination. Figure 21 illustrates three examples in which $N = 5$.

As before, the records of each entry are compiled on the summary sheet, and totals are achieved in the standard man-

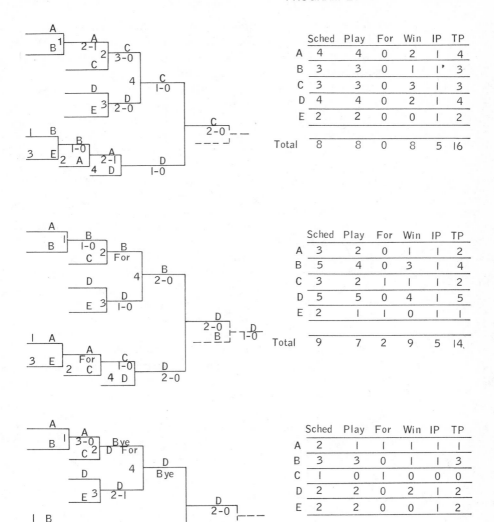

Figure 21.

ner. In checking relationship I, care must be taken to insure the use of the correct formula for double elimination play. If the final game is not played, the formula for the number of games in double elimination play is $2N - 2$. When the final game is played, the formula is $2N - 1$. In Example (A), the arithmetical total of games (8) equals the formula total $(2N - 2 = 8)$. In Example (B), the arithmetical total of games (9) equals the formula total $(2N - 1 = 9)$. The other two relationships are satisfied also in both examples.

Example (C) involves a double forfeit in the upper bracket. Entries A and C double-forfeit to create a bye in the fourth round. Also, two byes must be placed in the lower bracket. Since both A and C lost game 2 in the upper bracket, no loser can be placed on line 2 of the lower bracket. Correspondingly, no entry lost game 4 in the upper bracket, so no loser can be placed on line 4 in the lower bracket.

Apparently, relationship I is not satisfied; the arithmetical total of scheduled games (5) does not equal the formula total of eight. However, the three missing games can be accounted for in the three byes that were injected into the bracket past the first round. Game 4 in the upper bracket and the second and third games in the lower bracket were never scheduled or played, as far as the records of the involved entries are concerned. For each bye injected beyond the first round, one fewer game than normal can be expected in the arithmetical total for scheduled games. Each double forfeit in the upper bracket results in three such games, so three games must be added to the arithmetical total to correspond to the number of games actually scheduled for the tournament. (Double forfeits in the lower bracket are handled in the same manner as those for single elimination play.)

Again, the arithmetical total of scheduled games is used in checking the other two relationships. Appropriately, there is one more forfeit than normal and one less win than normal.

Statistics for Meets

Statistics for meets are easy. All one need do is list the entries on the summary sheet and add up individual and total participation. The numbers for scheduled and played games are handled as shown on the cover sheet (Fig. 22). The final packet consists only of cover sheet and summaries.

PROGRAM CONCLUSION

For organizations, figures are transferred to the filed entry form (Fig. 23) so that the awarding of points in the all-year

Wichita State University
Intramural Athletics

Activity Summary Sheet

Cross-Country
1973

Division	Season	Type Tour	Entries	Contests Sched	Contests Played	Per cent Played	Indiv Part.	Total Part.
Ungrad Men	Oct 20	meet	29	1	1	100	29	29
Ungrad Men								
Grad-Fac Men	Oct 20	meet	8	1	1	100	8	8
Grad-Fac Women								
Fraternity	Oct 20	meet	10	1	1	100	10	10
Totals			47	3	3	100	47	47

Division	Champion
Ungrad Men	Ken Wee
Ungrad Women	
Grad-Fac Men	Pat Blanchard
Grad-Fac Women	
Fraternity	Dennis Patterson

Comparison with Last Year	1972	1973	Inc.-Dec.	Per cent Inc.-Dec.
Entries	50	47	-3	-6
Contests Scheduled	3	3	0	0
Contests Played	3	3	0	0
Per cent Played	100	100	0	0
Individual Participation	50	47	-3	-6
Total Participation	50	47	-3	-6

Notes:

Figure 22.

point plan can be properly administered. Actually, this is done at the conclusion of each sport during the course of the year.

After all sports are completed, the end-of-the-year summaries are drawn (Fig. 24). These are what intramural directors take to their superiors in order to get better facilities, more funds, and a larger staff.

ORG. *PHI DELTA THETA*

Sport	Name	Phone	S	P	F	W	MP	EP	TP	IP	TP
Tennis Doubles	Jim Harris / Maru Jones	20 30	3	2	1	0	0	0	0	2	4
Horse-Shoes											
Wrestling											
128	Horace Helms	20 30	1	1	0	0	0	5	5	1	1
135											
142											
150	Harry Stuart	20 30	5	5	0	4	20	5	25	1	5
158	Joe Jackson	20 30	2	1	0	1	5	5	10	1	1
167	George Farley	20 30	2	2	0	1	5	5	10	1	2
176	Hal Edison	20 30	3	2	1	2	10	0	10	1	2
Unlimited											
Alt. 1											
2											
3											

Figure 23. Filed entry form.

Penn State University
Summary of Intramural Activities – 1970-71

	Closing Date for Entry	Season	Type Tourn.	Entries (*Denotes team)					Contests Scheduled	Contests Played	Individual Participation	Total Part.
				Frat.	Dorm.	Ind.	Grad.	Total				
Touch Football	Oct 1	Oct 5 Nov 22	R.R.	*50	99	61	23	233	726	681	5030	18,599
Golf-Medal	Oct 8	Oct 3-4 Oct 10-11	36 H. Medal	72	89	0	x	173	2	2	87	87
Tennis-Singles	Oct 1	Oct 9 Nov 10	S.E.	80	145	20	14	259	255	238	244	476
Bowling	Oct 8	Oct 14 Mar 16	R.R.	*45	86	13	0	144	914	893	1665	8889
Basketball	Oct 29	Nov 9 Mar 15	R.R.	*47	98	54	26	225	901	835	3314	12,841
Wrestling	Feb 18	Feb 24 Mar 12	S.E.	211	252	35	x	498	474	370	424	740
Handball-Singles	Jan 14	Jan 19 Feb 17	S.E. R.R.	106	171	16	14	307	332	296	281	592
Paddleball	Feb 4	Feb 10 Mar 15	S.E. R.R.	108	194	18	15	335	367	310	296	620
Handball-Doubles	Feb 4	Feb 17 Mar 15	S.E. R.R.	*64	88	10	6	168	186	132	262	528
Volleyball	Apr 8	Apr 13 May 25	R.R.	*45	90	20	15	170	424	355	1909	5003
Swimming	Apr 8	Apr 14 May 19	S.E.	*36	48	0	x	84	82	67	569	896
Badminton	Apr 8	Apr 15 May 12	S.E. R.R.	86	144	3	7	240	252	215	212	430
Tennis-Doubles	Apr 15	Apr 20 June 1	S.E. R.R.	*41	64	10	6	121	127	118	228	472
Golf-Team	Apr 15	Apr 20 June 8	S.E.	*37	51	0	x	88	86	80	410	800
Soccer	Apr 22	Apr 29 June 8	R.R.	*40	75	23	9	147	281	263	1734	4313
Horseshoes	May 6	May 17 June 2	R.R.	*35	54	3	x	92	157	110	168	440
Track	May 20	June 1, 2,3	Meets	*29	53	Ind. 15	x	82	3	3	261	430
									5569	4968		56,116

17 Activities

Male Student Enrollment (Spring Term)
Undergraduate 13,664   Graduate 3527

x = not offered for grad. students

Figure 24. *Continued on the following page.*

INTRAMURAL PROGRAM - 1970-71

COMPARISON WITH LAST YEAR

ACTIVITY	1969-70	1970-71	INC. DEC.	PERCENT INC.-DEC.
TOUCH FOOTBALL				
Entries	223	223	+ 10	+ 4.4%
Contests Sched.	684	726	+ 42	+ 6.1%
Contests Played	648	681	+ 33	+ 5.1%
Individual Part.	5099	5030	- 57	- 1.1%
Total Part.	17917	18599	+ 682	+ 3.8%
GOLF-MEDAL				
Entries	178	173	- 5	- 2.8%
Contests Sched.	2	2	-	-
Contests Played	2	2	-	-
Individual Part.	91	87	- 4	- 4.4%
Total Part.	91	87	- 4	- 4.4%
TENNIS-SINGLES				
Entries	276	259	- 17	- 6.1%
Contests Sched.	272	255	- 17	- 6.3%
Contests Played	240	238	- 2	- 0.8%
Individual Part.	253	244	- 9	- 3.6%
Total Part.	480	476	- 4	- 0.8%
PADDLEBALL-SINGLES				
Entries	317	335	+ 18	+ 5.7%
Contests Sched.	331	367	+ 36	+ 10.9%
Contests Played	275	310	+ 35	+ 12.7%
Individual Part.	273	296	+ 28	+ 8.4%
Total Part.	550	620	+ 70	+ 12.7%
HANDBALL-SINGLES				
Entries	280	307	+ 27	+ 9.6%
Contests Sched.	297	332	+ 35	+ 11.8%
Contests Played	261	296	+ 35	+ 13.4%
Individual Part.	253	281	+ 28	+ 11.1%
Total Part.	522	592	+ 70	+ 13.4%

1969-70	1970-71	INC. DEC.	PERCENT INC.-DEC.	ACTIVITY
				BOWLING
155	144	- 11	- 7.1%	Entries
955	914	- 41	- 4.3%	Contests Sched.
918	893	- 25	- 2.7%	Contests Played
1853	1665	- 188	- 10.1%	Individual Part.
9027	8889	- 138	- 1.5%	Total Part.
				VOLLEYBALL
161	170	+ 9	+ 5.6%	Entries
383	424	+ 41	+ 10.7%	Contests Sched.
312	355	+ 43	+ 13.8%	Contests Played
1825	1909	+ 84	+ 4.6%	Individual Part.
4647	5003	+ 356	+ 7.7%	Total Part.
				BADMINTON
223	240	+ 17	+ 7.6%	Entries
244	252	+ 8	+ 3.3%	Contests Sched.
194	215	+ 21	+ 10.8%	Contests Played
187	212	+ 25	+ 13.4%	Individual Part.
388	430	+ 42	+ 10.8%	Total Part.
				TENNIS-DOUBLES
124	121	- 3	- 2.4%	Entries
130	127	- 3	- 2.3%	Contests Sched.
117	118	+ 1	+ 0.8%	Contests Played
232	228	- 4	- 1.7%	Individual Part.
468	472	+ 4	+ 0.8%	Total Part.
				GOLF-TEAM
96	88	- 8	- 8.3%	Entries
94	86	- 8	- 8.5%	Contests Sched.
85	80	- 5	- 5.8%	Contests Played
440	410	- 30	- 6.8%	Individual Part.
850	800	- 50	- 5.8%	Total Part.

Figure 24. *Continued on opposite page.*

SWIMMING

Entries	94	84	– 10	– 10.6%
Contests Sched.	91	82	– 9	– 9.9%
Contests Played	66	67	+ 1	+ 1.5%
Individual Part.	529	569	+ 40	+ 7.6%
Total Part.	848	896	+ 48	+ 5.7%

BASKETBALL

Entries	226	225	– 1	– 0.4%
Contests Sched.	876	901	+ 25	+ 2.9%
Contests Played	786	835	+ 49	+ 6.2%
Individual Part.	3395	3314	– 81	– 2.4%
Total Part.	12160	12841	+ 681	+ 5.6%

HANDBALL–DOUBLES

Entries	154	168	+ 14	+ 9.1%
Contests Sched.	157	186	+ 29	+ 18.5%
Contests Played	141	132	– 9	– 6.4%
Individual Part	278	262	– 16	– 5.8%
Total Part.	564	528	– 36	– 6.4%

WRESTLING

Entries	467	498	+ 11	+ 2.2%
Contests Sched.	464	474	+ 10	+ 2.0%
Contests Played	374	370	– 4	– 1.1%
Individual Part.	409	424	+ 15	+ 3.7%
Total Part.	748	740	– 8	– 1.1%

SUMMARY

	1969-70	1970-71
TOTAL CONTESTS SCHED.	5,360	5,569
TOTAL CONTESTS PLAYED	4,753	4,968
PERCENT PLAYED	88.6%	89.2%

SOCCER

Entries	125	147	+ 22	+ 17.6%
Contests Sched.	237	281	+ 44	+ 18.5%
Contests Played	222	263	+ 41	+ 18.5%
Individual Part.	1532	1734	+ 202	+ 13.2%
Total Part.	3677	4313	+ 636	+ 17.3%

HORSESHOES–DOUBLES

Entries	82	92	+ 10	+ 12.2%
Contests Sched.	140	157	+ 17	+ 12.1%
Contests Played	109	110	+ 1	+ 0.9%
Individual Part.	158	168	+ 10	+ 6.3%
Total Part.	436	440	+ 4	+ 0.9%

TRACK

Entries	87	82	– 5	– 5.7%
Contests Sched.	3	3	–	–
Contests Played	3	3	–	–
Individual Part.	324	261	– 63	– 19.4%
Total Part.	531	430	– 101	– 19.0%

PERCENTAGE OF SCHEDULED CONTESTS ACTUALLY PLAYED

Touch Football	95.2%	Bowling	97.7%
Golf-Medal	100.0%	Volleyball	83.5%
Tennis-Singles	93.3%	Badminton	85.3%
Paddleball	84.5%	Tennis-Doubles	92.9%
Handball-Singles	89.2%	Golf-Team	93.0%
Swimming	81.7%	Basketball	93.6%
Basketball	92.7%	Soccer	70.0%
Handball-Doubles	71.0%	Horseshoes	70.0%
		Track	100.0%

ALL SPORTS 89.2%

DORMITORY	89.7%	(Played 2522 of 2812 Sched.)
FRATERNITY	89.0%	(Played 1492 of 1677 Sched.)
INDEPENDENT	87.0%	(Played 616 of 708 Sched.)
GRADUATE	91.1%	(Played 349 of 382 Sched.)

Figure 24. Continued.

Program Guidelines

WICHITA STATE UNIVERSITY
INTRAMURAL GUIDELINES
Frank Rokosz, Director

DIVISIONS OF COMPETITION

(1) undergraduate men   (2) fraternity   (3) women
(4) grad-faculty men   (5) co-ed

Separate competition is provided for each division, and each division has its own champion. The photographs of division winners appear in the intramural display case in the CAC.

CONDITIONS OF PARTICIPATION

Both undergraduate and graduate students must be enrolled for a minimum of three credits. Faculty participation is limited to those who are officially paid and recognized by the university. No guest lecturers.

Members of varsity squads may not compete in that particular intramural sport or its associate. The active squad rosters on the date of the first varsity contest in a sport shall be used to determine intramural eligibility. Any man or woman who works out with a squad and/or retains a locker and equipment on or after the date of the first varsity contest shall be considered ineligible for the entire intramural season in that sport. Anyone who has been declared a professional in a sport may not compete in the intramural sport.

Varsity athletes may compete in their intramural sports only after a one-year absence from varsity competition.

An individual may play for only one team per sport. Individuals are not permitted to switch from one team to another during the course of a season. The first team that a player represents is the only team for which he is eligible to play.

In league or championship play-offs, teams cannot use players who have not played in at least one regular season contest for that team.

An individual who uses an assumed name or plays under the name of another student is not permitted to participate further in the intramural program.

A team forfeits any contest in which an ineligible player participates.

Teams guilty of frequent forfeitures might not be permitted to enter subsequent tournaments.

POSTPONEMENTS — FORFEITS

Absolutely no changes in schedule are permitted in those sports where officials are required. Once a schedule is printed, that is it. Requests for postponements are not honored. Exception: should two teams agree to play at a time other than the one that is scheduled, they shall do so with their own officials. For individual or dual contests, scheduled matches may be rearranged by mutual consent of opponents as long as matches are played before the next scheduled contest. The intramural office must approve any postponement and subsequent arrangement.

Ten minutes after the scheduled time of a contest, a forfeit is awarded to the team or individual ready to play.

PROTESTS

Questions that arise on the court or field of play concerning rules and interpretations, officiating procedures, etc., are decided immediately by the intramural supervisor on duty. Right or wrong, the decisions of the supervisor are final. When significant questions arise, team captains may request of the official a halt in play so the intramural supervisor may be consulted. Officials are instructed to consult with supervisors whenever they are unsure of a rule.

Only those protests involving player ineligibility are considered after a contest is completed. Protests of that sort must be made within 24 hours of the completion of the contest.

RECOGNITION

An all-year award is presented to the fraternity which accumulates the most points under the point award plan.

Photographs of division winners of each sport are taken and placed in the intramural display case in the CAC. Photographs and news items also appear in the *Sunflower.*

DEPOSITION OF INFORMATION

Entry information is sent by flyer to all organizations with mailing addresses. Intramural calendar posters pervade the campus. Announcements and intramural results also appear in the *Sunflower.* Information may always be obtained at the intramural office, 102 Henrion Gym. Phone: 689-3340.

ENTRY PROCEDURE

All entries are made at the intramural office, 102 Henrion Gym. No entries are accepted by phone. Entry deadlines are established for each tournament. Late entries are accepted only if the schedule has not yet been established. A late entry fee is required if entry is accepted.

Forfeit fees for certain sports are also collected at time of entry. The fees are returned at the season's end to those teams which have not forfeited more than once. The fees collected from teams which have forfeited twice or more are retained by the intramural office.

Rosters are not required at time of entry for team sports.

SCHEDULING

In those team sports where round robin scheduling is appropriate, all teams in all divisions play the same number of games. Perfect round robin scheduling is not always possible, so some leagues must play round robin plus a partial round robin. This means that each team plays the other teams at least once and a given number of teams more than once. The extra pairings are determined by random draw.

INJURIES

The university is not responsible for injuries or accidents that occur during intramural contests. Intramural supervisors will perform first aid when necessary and refer the injured person to either the student health center or Wesley Medical Center.

Calendar of Events

WICHITA STATE UNIVERSITY
INTRAMURAL CALENDAR 1974–75

Activity	Entry Deadline	Entry Fee	Late Entry Fee	Forfeit Fee	Dates of Play	Times of Day
Softball	Fri Aug 30	$1.00	$5.00	$5.00	Mon–Thurs	4, 5, 6 PM
Tennis	Fri Aug 30	$ .25	$1.00		Sat Sept 7 Sun Sept 8	afternoon & evening
Bicycle Sprint	Wed Sept 18				Sun Sept 22	6:30 PM
				Rain date	Sun Sept 29	6:30 PM
Touch Football	Wed Sept 25	$1.00	$5.00	$5.00	Mon–Thur	4, 5 PM
Cross-country	Wed Oct 2				Sun Oct 6	6:30 PM
				Rain date	Sun Oct 13	6:30 PM
Pistol	Wed Oct 16	$1.00			Sun Oct 20	6:30 PM
Badminton (singles and doubles)	Wed Oct 16	$ .25	$1.00		Mon–Thur	7–10 PM
Volleyball	Wed Oct 30	$1.00	$5.00	$5.00	Mon–Thur	6:30–10 PM
Riflery	Wed Oct 30	$1.00			Sun Nov 3	6:30 PM
Wrestling	Wed Nov 6	$ .25	$1.00		Nov 14, 19, 21, 26	6:30 PM
Pool	Wed Nov 6	$ .25	$1.00		Sun Nov 17	6:00 PM
Table tennis (singles and doubles)	Wed Nov 20	$ .25	$1.00		Sun Nov 24	6:30 PM
Gymnastics	Wed Nov 20				Sat Dec 7	9:30 AM
Basketball	Wed Jan 22	$1.00	$5.00	$5.00	Sun–Fri	6:30–10 PM
Pistol	Wed Jan 22	$1.00			Sun Jan 26	6:30 PM
Bowling	Wed Jan 29				Sun Feb 2	7:00 PM
Foul shooting	Wed Feb 12				Sun Feb 16	7:00 PM
Riflery	Wed Feb 19	$1.00			Sun Feb 23	6:30 PM
Fencing	Wed Mar 26				Sun Mar 30	6:30 PM
Archery	Wed Mar 26				Sun Mar 30	6:30 PM
Swimming	Wed Apr 2				Apr 6, 7, 8, 9	6:30 PM
Golf	Wed Apr 2	$ .25			Apr 12, 13, 19	1:00 PM
Track and Field	Wed Apr 16				Apr 20–24	6:30 PM
Tennis	Fri Apr 18	$ .25	$1.00		Sat Apr 26, Sun Apr 27	afternoon & evening

Divisions of competition: undergrad men, fraternity, women, grad-fac men, and co-ed.

Entry period begins one week before the deadline date. Deadlines are at 4:00 PM and are met at the intramural office, 102 Henrion Gym. Entry and forfeit fees are collected at time of entry. Forfeit fee is retained by the intramural office at the occurrence of a team's second forfeit.

POINT SYSTEM

WICHITA STATE UNIVERSITY
FRATERNITY POINT SYSTEM

TEAM SPORTS

Category A: Two teams per fraternity in fraternity division.

Tournament	No-Forfeit Bonus Points	Victory Points (per game)	Championship Points	
			Champion	Runner-up
6-man football	25	10	100	60
Basketball	25	10	100	60

Category B: One team per fraternity in fraternity division.

Tournament	No-Forfeit Bonus Points	Victory Points	Championship Points	
			Champion	Runner-up
Volleyball	25	10 per match	100	60
Softball	25	10 per game	100	60

Category C: Two men per fraternity in each event in the fraternity division.

Tournament	No-Forfeit Bonus Points	Victory Points	Championship Points	
			Champion	Runner-up
Swimming and diving	5 per man	see below	100	60
Track and field	5 per man	see below	100	60

Points for each place finish are added toward a team total.

Place	1	2	3	4	5
Points	10	8	6	4	2

EVENTS

Swimming and Diving	Track and Field
50-yd free style	100-yd dash
100-yd free style	220-yd dash
50-yd back stroke	440-yd dash
50-yd breast stroke	mile run
50-yd butterfly	440-yd relay
100-yd individual medley	880-yd relay
200-yd free style relay	shot put
diving	high jump
	long jump

DUAL SPORTS

Two teams per fraternity in fraternity division.

Tournament	No-Forfeit Bonus Points	Victory Points (per match)	Championship Points	
			Champion	Runner-up
Table tennis	10	5	25	15
Badminton	10	5	25	15

INDIVIDUAL SPORTS

Three men per fraternity in fraternity division.

Tournament	No-Forfeit Bonus Points	Victory Points	Championship Points	
			Champion	Runner-up
Fall tennis	5	5 per match	25	15
Spring tennis	5	5 per match	25	15
Badminton	5	5 per match	25	15
Table tennis	5	5 per match	25	15
Pool	5	5 per match	50	30
Wrestling	5	{ 5 per pin / 3 per decision	20	10

		Places	Points
Cross-country	5	1	50
Bicycle sprint	5	2	30
Golf	5	3	25
Bowling	5	4	20
Foul shooting	5	5	15
		6	10
		7	8
		8	6
		9	4
		10	2

Answers to
Chapter Problems

CHAPTER EIGHT

1. Single elimination draw for 19 entries.

19	rounds = 5	1st rd. gms. = 3
10–9		
5–5–5–4	games = 18	byes = 13
3–2–3–2–3–2–2–2		

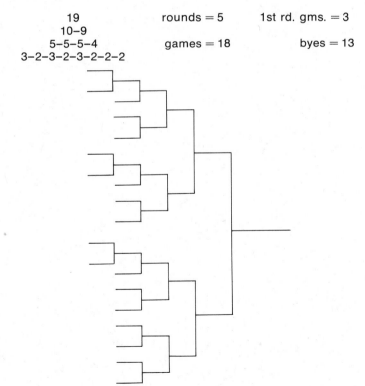

2. Single elimination draw for 54 entries.

```
            54                    rounds = 6        1st rd. gms. = 22
          27–27
       14–13–14–13              games = 53              byes = 10
      7–7–7–6–7–7–7–6
4–3–4–3–4–3–3–3–4–3–4–3–4–3–3–3
```

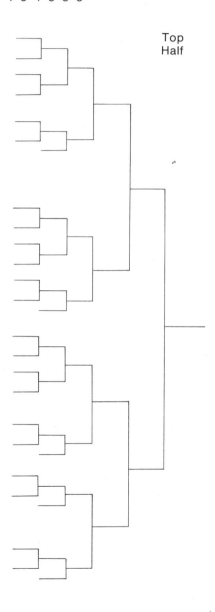

Top
Half

3. $N = 20$ 5 seeds are desired

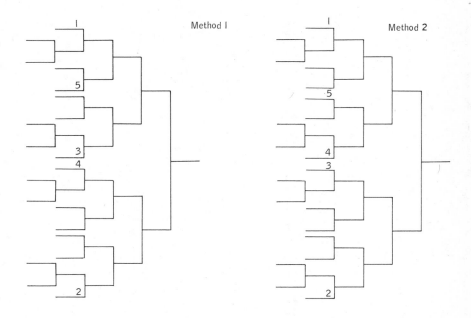

4. a. 8 days   b. 16 days   c. 4 days   d. 12 days   e. 14 days

5. a. 6 g/d   b. 6 g/d   c. impossible d. 3 g/d

6. a. $N = 36$ b. $N = 16$ c. $N = 73$ d. $N = 22$

CHAPTER NINE

1. a. Double elimination draw for 22 entries.

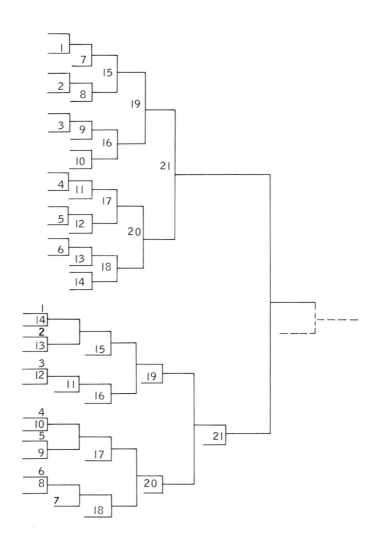

b. Double elimination draw for six entries.

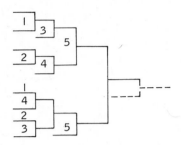

2. a. $N = 11$ games $= 21$

round	1	2	3	4	5	6	7	8	9
games	3	3	4	4	2	2	1	1	1

b. $N = 23$ games $= 45$

round	1	2	3	4	5	6	7	8	9	10	11
games	7	7	8	8	4	4	2	2	1	1	1

c. $N = 7$ games $= 13$

round	1	2	3	4	5	6	7
games	3	3	2	2	1	1	1

3. a. 18 days   b. 11 days   c. 20 days   d. 18 days

4. a. 8 g/d   b. impossible   c. 5 g/d   d. 3 g/d

5. a. $N = 22$ b. $N = 66$ c. $N = 8$ (at 4 g/d)   d. $N = 13$

CHAPTER TEN

1. a. Type I consolation draw for 18 entries.

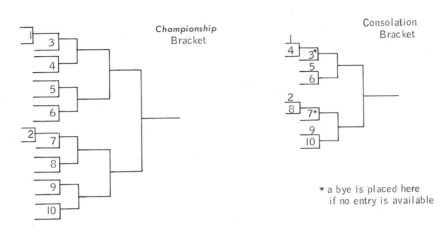

*a bye is placed here
if no entry is available

b. Type I consolation draw for 23 entries.

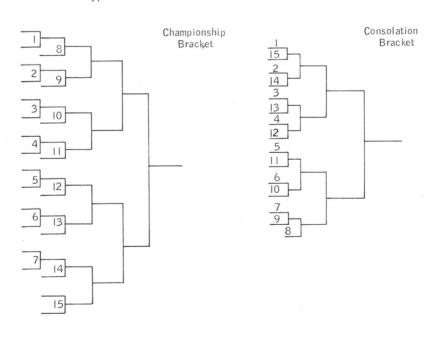

2. a. 9 games   b. 52 games   c. 30 games

3. a.

round	1	2	3	4	5	6
games	9	8	8	8	4	2

b.

round	1	2	3	4	5
games	5	5	8	4	2

c.

round	1	2	3	4
games	4	4	4	2

4. a. 5 days   b. 18 days   c. 14 days   d. 26 days

5. a. 5 g/d   b. impossible   c. 13 g/d   d. 2 g/d

6. a. $N = 10$ (at 4 g/d)   b. $N = 14$ c. $N = 65$ d. $N = 28$

CHAPTER ELEVEN

1. a. Type II consolation draw for 19 entries.

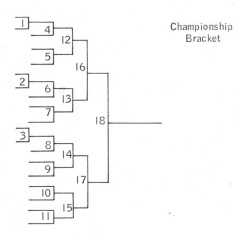

Championship
Bracket

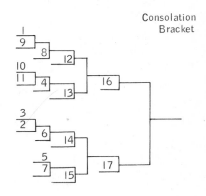

Consolation
Bracket

b. Type II consolation draw for 24 entries.

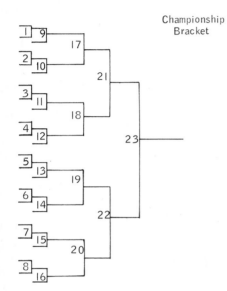

Championship
Bracket

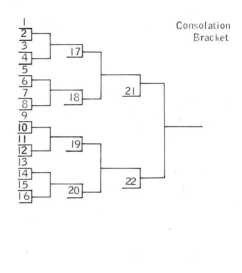

Consolation
Bracket

2. a.

round	1	2	3	4	5	6	7
games	4	8	8	4	4	2	2

b.

round	1	2	3	4	5	6	7	8
games	11	11	8	8	4	4	2	2

c.

round	1	2	3	4	5	6	7	8	9	10
games	10	10	16	16	8	8	4	4	2	2

3. a. 12 days   b. 6 days   c. 8 days   d. 10 days

4. a. 8 g/d   b. impossible   c. 12 g/d   d. impossible

5. a. $N = 10$ (at 4 g/d)   b. $N = 34$ c. $N = 35$ d. $N = 56$

CHAPTER TWELVE

1. a. Bagnall-Wild tournament draw for 17 entries.

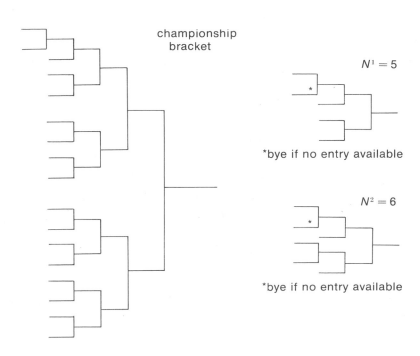

championship
bracket

$N^1 = 5$

*bye if no entry available

$N^2 = 6$

*bye if no entry available

b. Bagnall-Wild tournament draw for 28 entries.

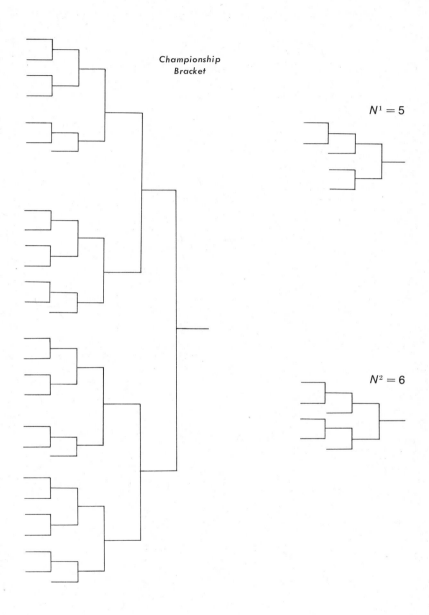

Championship
Bracket

$N^1 = 5$

$N^2 = 6$

2. a. 13 days   b. 9 days   c. 12 days   d. 14 days

CHAPTER THIRTEEN

1. a. Mueller-Anderson Playback tournament draw for 13 entries.

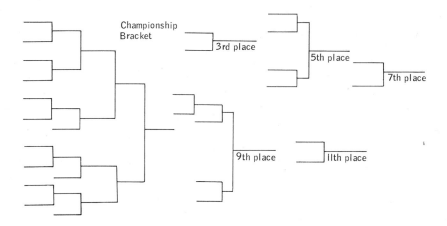

b. Mueller-Anderson Playback draw for 26 entries.

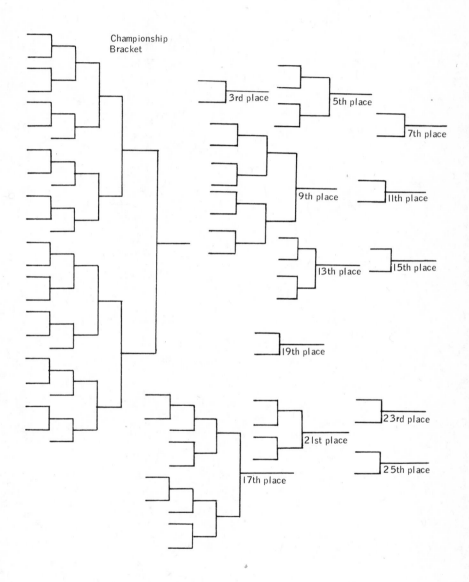

CHAPTER FOURTEEN

1. Triple elimination tournament draw for 17 entries.

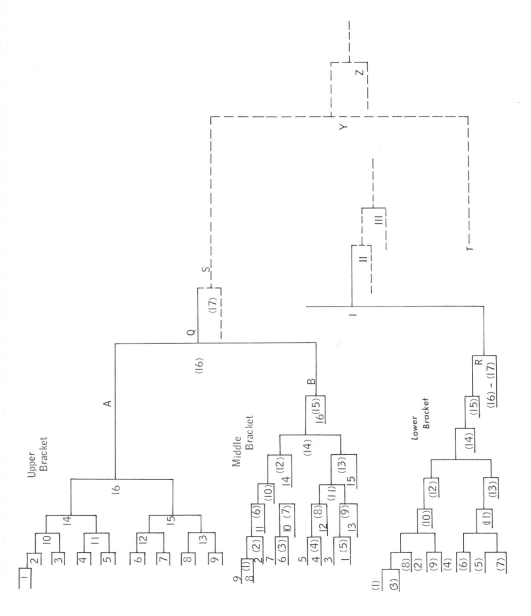

2. a. 16 days   b. 11 days   c. 17 days   d. 23 days

CHAPTER FIFTEEN

1. a. 115 games   b. 225 games   c. 211 games

2.

rd. 1	rd. 2	rd. 3	rd. 4	rd. 5	rd. 6	rd. 7	rd. 8	rd. 9
1–10	1–9	1–8	1–7	1–6	1–5	1–4	1–3	1–2
2–9	10–8	9–7	8–6	7–5	6–4	5–3	4–2	3–10
3–8	2–7	10–6	9–5	8–4	7–3	6–2	5–10	4–9
4–7	3–6	2–5	10–4	9–3	8–2	7–10	6–9	5–8
5–6	4–5	3–4	2–3	10–2	9–10	8–9	7–8	6–7

X	A	B	C	D	E	F	G	H	I	J
A	X	1	2	3	4	5	6	7	8	9
B		X	3	4	5	6	7	8	9	2
C			X	5	6	7	8	9	1	4
D				X	7	8	9	1	2	6
E					X	9	1	2	3	8
F						X	2	3	4	1
G							X	4	5	3
H								X	6	5
I									X	7
J										X

3.

rd. 1	rd. 2	rd. 3	rd. 4	rd. 5	rd. 6	rd. 7	rd. 8
B–1	B–2	B–3	B–4	B–5	B–6	B–7	B–8
I–2	I–3	I–4	I–5	I–6	I–7	I–8	I–1
II–3	II–4	II–5	II–6	II–7	II–8	II–1	II–2
III–4	III–5	III–6	III–7	III–8	III–1	III–2	III–3
IV–5	IV–6	IV–7	IV–8	IV–1	IV–2	IV–3	IV–4
V–6	V–7	V–8	V–1	V–2	V–3	V–4	V–5
VI–7	VI–8	VI–1	VI–2	VI–3	VI–4	VI–5	VI–6
VII–8	VII–1	VII–2	VII–3	VII–4	VII–5	VII–6	VII–7

4.

rd. 1	rd. 2	rd. 3	rd. 4	rd. 5	rd. 6
B–9	B–8	B–7	B–6	B–5	B–4
1–8	9–7	8–6	7–5	6–4	5–3
2–7	1–6	9–5	8–4	7–3	6–2
3–6	2–5	1–4	9–3	8–2	7–1
4–5	3–4	2–3	1–2	9–1	8–9

rd. 7	rd. 8	rd. 9	One Partial Rd. Rob.	
B–3	B–2	B–1	1–8	5–3
4–2	3–1	2–9*	9–7	4–2
5–1	4–9	3–8	8–6	3–1
6–9	5–8	4–7	7–5	2–9*
7–8	6–7	5–6	6–4	

5.

TEAM	W	L	%	G.B.
Zeros	62	10	.861	—
Stars	35	20	.636	18½
Dons	28	27	.509	25½
Colts	25	40	.385	33½
Masons	19	51	.271	42

6. a. 18 games   b. 14 games

7. a. impossible   b. 10 lgs. of 4 and 2 lgs. of 5
   c. 2 lgs. of 10 and 1 lg. of 9   d. 15 lgs. of 4 and 1 lg. of 5

8. a. 47 days, 11 weeks and 3 days, play ends on Thursday of the 12th week.
   b. 19 days, 4 weeks and 3 days, play ends on Monday of the 5th week.
   c. 11 days, 2 weeks and 3 days, play ends on Wednesday of the 3rd week.
   d. 24 days, 6 weeks, play ends on Wednesday of the 6th week.

9. a. 7 g/d   b. 13 g/d   c. 11 g/d   d. 6 g/d

10. a. $N = 72$ b. $N = 96$ c. $N = 84$ d. $N = 192$

°Top two seeded entries play twice.

BIBLIOGRAPHY

Beeman, Harris F., Carol A. Harding, and James H. Humphrey. *Intramural Sports: A Text and Study Guide,* 3rd Edition. Dubuque, Iowa: William C. Brown Company, Publishers, 1974.

Hyatt, Ronald W. *Intramural Sports Programs: Their Organization and Administration.* St. Louis: The C. V. Mosby Company. In preparation.

Kleindienst, Viola, and Arthur Weston. *Intramural and Recreation Programs for Schools and Colleges.* New York: Appleton-Century-Crofts, 1964.

Means, Louis E. *Intramurals: Their Organization and Administration,* 2nd Edition. Englewood Cliffs, New Jersey: Prentice-Hall, Inc., 1974.

Mueller, Pat. *Intramurals: Programming and Administration,* 4th Edition. New York: The Ronald Press Company, 1971.

INDEX

Italicized numbers refer to illustrations.

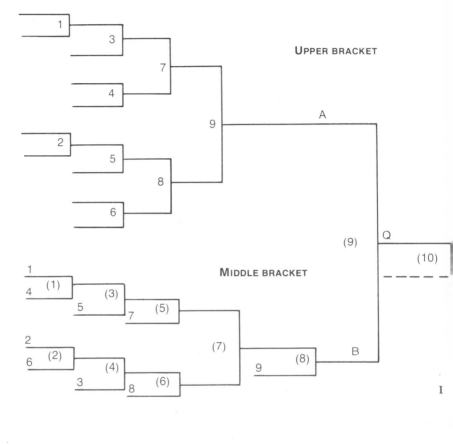

UPPER BRACKET

MIDDLE BRACKET

I

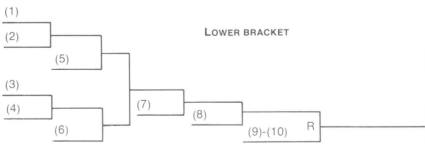

LOWER BRACKET